POPULAR FLOWERING SHRUBS

Also by H. L. V. Fletcher

GARDENING IN WINDOW BOXES
AND OTHER CONTAINERS

POPULAR FLOWERING PLANTS

POPULAR FLOWERING SHRUBS

H. L. V. FLETCHER

PELHAM BOOKS

First published in Great Britain by
PELHAM BOOKS LTD
52 Bedford Square
London, W.C.1
1971

7207 0462 6

Set and printed in Great Britain by
Tonbridge Printers Ltd, Peach Hall Works, Tonbridge, Kent
in Bembo twelve on thirteen point, on paper
supplied by P. F. Bingham Ltd, and bound by
James Burn at Esher, Surrey

CONTENTS

ILLUSTRATIONS

FOREWORD

I gave this book its brief title because I did not want one that was too cumbersome, but I have felt at liberty to include a few shrubs that are grown mainly for leaf colour, also some that are valued more for their berries than for their flowers.

As usual Mr C. W. Newman, our Radnorshire librarian, and his staff have been most helpful in finding any book I wanted for reference.

I want to thank also the Wyevale Nurseries, Hereford, who kindly gave me permission to go into their nurseries at any time to photograph shrubs. Apart from a few taken in the Oxford Botanic Gardens my photographs for this book were taken either at Wyevale or in my own garden.

I want to thank my wife for typing the manuscript and my cousin, Miss Martha Knowles, for correcting the proofs for me.

H. L. V. Fletcher

Chapter 1: SHRUBBERY OR SHRUB GARDEN?

The Victorians were an odd lot. Or so we are told. As the twentieth century rolls on they fade further away into the distance; a sort of nostalgia is gathering around them and some of them are becoming almost romantic figures – Forsytes and such like. We may yet see them as picturesque as the Cavaliers and Roundheads, who in fact treated each other in a most unromantic murderous way. But for the moment their oddness remains.

They wore long dresses and the most laughable suits (according to sex), they sent little boys up dreadful chimneys and little girls down coal mines. The Lower Classes drank gin to excess. The men drank too much beer, which was too cheap to be respectable, and they got drunk and beat their wives. Woman's Place Was In The Home and the men would not allow them to vote. They believed in God and going to Church and the Ten Commandments, though not to the extent of obeying them all. They believed in Heaven and quite a few believed in Hell. They did not believe in divorce – well not for respectable people; nor, openly, in birth control, and a lot of other necessities (by our standards) which it was not even decent to mention – and they thought Being Respectable was important. Good children were seen and not heard and bad children were also seen and not heard because they were beaten if they did not obey the rules – their parents never having heard of child psychologists. I could continue in this vein for a whole chapter at least.

The reason for all this remembrance of things past is that

Victorian gardens were noted for a dreadful feature called the Shrubbery. It was a dismal affair. If you want to recapture the mood look up the first verse of the fourth part of Tennyson's *Lady of Shallot:*

> In the stormy east-wind straining,
> The pale yellow woods were waning,
> The broad stream in his banks complaining,
> Heavily the low sky raining
>   Over tower'd Camelot.

Hardy got it more briefly:

> When beeches drip in browns and duns,
> And thresh, and ply.

The Victorian Shrubbery was most dismal, damp, dank, dark. Gloomy Laurels and other unspeakable evergreens on which the rain fell unceasingly, and on which the sun never shone.

An aura of despair surrounded it.

It wouldn't have mattered, but the result for many of us was that Shrubbery became a Dirty Word, and a place where the murdered person was deposited.

And was it true? Of course not. I don't believe a word of it.

Admittedly the Victorian gardeners did realise more than earlier gardeners the value of shrubs, either individually, or grouped together for decorative effect in large gardens. The fashion was given impetus by the discoveries that were made by the nineteenth century plant hunters, Wilson, Forrest, Robert Fortune and many others, but some beautiful species of the plants they discovered were already in cultivation. Lilac (Gerard's 'White and Blue Pipe Privet') is illustrated in a book, Mathiolus's *Commentarii*, published in 1565. Mock Orange was here before 1597: Gerard had it in 'Great plentie' in his garden, Rhododendrons (not the multitude of species we have today) were described by an Italian botanist about 1583 and Magnolias by the Spanish physician Francisco Hernandez.

Apart from the introductions from other parts of the world

there were our own native shrubs, a part of literature as much as of gardening – Roses, above all Roses, and Honeysuckle; the Guelder Rose and the Wild Cherry; Crab Apples and Gorse and Heathers.

Oh, there was no shortage of material. Not the embarrassment of choice that faces us today, but no shortage. Gardening developed from the culture of food, and then herbs for medicine. Culture for decoration came later and by degrees. John Evelyn wrote one of the best books ever on trees (*Sylva, A Discourse on Forest Trees*) but though he was an excellent gardener and had an excellent garden, including by the way a magnificent Holly hedge, he was interested in trees as material for timber.

There is in existence a letter he wrote to Pepys (September 1, 1686) asking him to pass on a list to a Captain he had met at dinner in Pepys's house. This man was going to command some forces in New England and had offered to try to get plants or seeds for Mr Evelyn. The list was composed solely of trees, except for Sarsaparilla (*sic*). He wanted 'The trees in Barills their rootes wraped in mosse . . . they will do well packed in matts, but the Barill is best.'

He wanted Tulip trees – certainly a flowering tree, but cultivated for timber – also some Sumachs. Otherwise, not a purely decorative shrub among them. The Shrubbery as such evidently had not yet arrived. John Rea's *Flora, Ceres et Pomona* (1676) contained a detailed account of how a nobleman's garden should be laid out. It would contain flower beds, fruit and 'a handsom octangular somer-house, roofed everyway and finely furnished with seats about and a table in the middle.'

No shrubs!

Perhaps that statement should be qualified. In some gardens small trees were grown not for their flowers but so that they could be trained and clipped into formal shapes: circles, pyramids and so on; or fantastic ones like knights on horseback, peacocks and heraldic beasts, done mainly with evergreens though such plants as thorn were used. This was topiary (*topiarius* – landscape gardening) and if it was not gardening on the highest level it was clever and needed patience. You either like this tranquil garden art very much or you loathe it like the devil hates a parson. Bacon was not very keen: 'I, for my part, do not like images cut out in Juniper, or other garden stuff: they be for children.' Not that Bacon's 'princely garden' would be everyone's taste. Addison and Steele, who seemed to prefer the simple to the formal, deplored having 'trees in the most awkward figures of men and animals, than in the most regular of their own,' and it was left to Pope, who had some ghastly features in his own plot – grottoes of clinker or whatnot – to deal topiary what should have been its death-blow in an imaginary, mocking catalogue:

> An old maid of honour in wormwood
> A quickset hog, shot up into a porcupine.
> A lavender pig with sage growing in his belly.

And so on.

It only remains to add that topiary, like many other garden arts condemned to die, stayed cheerfully alive. You can see many a mounted horseman or peacock or animal growing in box or cypress in many a roadside cottage garden while there are gardens of great houses where the topiary is (or lately was) very fine indeed.

No gardening fashion comes overnight like a raised or a dropped hemline: it creeps like ink spilled on blotting paper, but to the Victorians should go most of the credit for recognising the value of shrubs in the garden.

So they had some good points after all, and if their colonists were occasionally a bit rough to the 'lesser breeds without the law' (writ sarcastic, please note!) they did look for beautiful flowers and they did introduce some into their gardens at home.

By the time we come to that irritable giant William Robinson, the choice was very wide indeed. He wrote *The English Flower Garden* and that is still a splendid guide. What he did not like he did not like and he said so, but his scorn did not destroy and luckily there were plenty of good shrubs he did admire.

I think shrub culture got into the doldrums early in this

century. Partly that was a reaction against the Victorian Shrubbery. Places like Bodnant, and Sir William Stern's Highdown always have given pride of place to splendid shrubs, but the majority of us have not Bodnants, or the acres of Wisley – nor, for that matter the money and labour to run them.

I know when I started on my pilgrimage with mattock, fork and spade I had no immediate urge to plant shrubs. I knew I must have a herbaceous border, a rose garden, a rock garden, even a pool, but though I had a good deal of ground (much of it rough) nobody urged shrubs on me.

They are certainly in fashion again today. Their popularity probably dates from between the two world wars when money to run large grounds was in short supply and labour to keep them in good condition was even shorter.

So the idea caught on that growing shrubs was a good way of having a pleasant garden that would not be too much trouble to keep in order. Not all shrubs were suitable, of course. Weeds will grow under a standard flowering Cherry as easily as they will down a row of carrots. But low spreading evergreens are bad company for almost any weeds, and quite a few deciduous subjects are discouraging, even to the strongest perennial weeds. I have a fine young *Magnolia soulangeana* for instance and it is bare all winter but it is so dense through spring and summer that even those pretty pests, the Celandines, have decided its shade is no home for them. My biggest winter flowering Jasmine sprawling heavily into a wide path also loses its leaves, but nothing wants to live under it. So if your main idea in growing shrubs is to save work, choose carefully. If possible visit either a good nursery or a garden such as Wisley where you can see shrubs growing and can decide if they will suit your purpose. Like my Magnolia and Winter Jasmine some leaf losers are excellent; others are not.

I'm not sure that planting shrubs solely to avoid doing any gardening is the nicest reason, not for dedicated gardeners anyhow. But a poor start is better than none at all and most people, once they discover that the Shrub Garden (a better title

than Shrubbery with its Laurel-haunted Victorian associations)
is a very fine garden on its own account, go on from the useful
to the beautiful and want the lot.

And another fashion has arrived: the use of ground-cover
plants. I don't know how it came or when it came, like Topsy in
Uncle Tom's Cabin it just growed. A few decades ago you never
heard the phrase: now it has its own literature, lots of articles and
at least a couple of books. All it means is that you grow dense
ground-covering flowering plants on all bare soil and so smother
or choke out all the weeds. Of course the principle has been there
all the time, only it never got recognition. My little stone sink
was planted a dozen or more years ago with close-growing
saxifrages and they completely cover it and I don't suppose I find
one weed a year in it. But it did not occur to me that I could
adapt the same idea to other parts of the garden.

Again, not all spreading plants are suitable. Not many weeds
will challenge the supremacy of a strong mat of London Pride,
but I have a dense colony of *Campanula poshcharskyana* on a bank
through which grass will grow happily. So you have to choose
carefully.

Then there are the plants you can grow among shrubs from
which you expect nothing but their beauty. Most of these are
bulbs and they should be grown mainly among the leaf-losers.
Not all bulbs do. Daffodils are better than Tulips but generally
speaking most of the spring-flowering bulbs are suitable. They
flower before the shrubs and give the garden colour and interest
at a time when, without them, it would be pretty quiet, even dull.
So you should plant lots of Daffodils, in little groups for preference,
a few Tulips (the species or wild types are useful here) in strategic
spots, and the smaller ones, Snowdrops, Crocuses, Scillas,
Chionodoxas, Muscari, some of the blue Anemones, *A. appenina*,
A. blanda, and lots of our wild Anemones (the bulb merchant will
have some improved types of these) in prominent positions where
they will not be overlooked. It is possible to make mistakes. I put
some *Anemone appenina* too close to some Daffodils and the
Daffodil leaves fall on them each year and smother the delicate

blue flowers. Keep the tall and the short well away from each other.

Also the small bulbs and the weed-smotherers are not always the best companions. Some bulbs thrust through anything; others are choked out much as the weeds are. I don't think the garden teachers have done their homework here, so you might need to do a bit of experimenting. I have masses of a large form of our native Anemone growing strongly among all sorts of carpeters in the rock garden – and very nice they look – but some of the winter-flowering Crocuses that got overgrown by a strong sedum are not at all happy.

Chapter 2: THE SITE

As a general rule growing shrubs does not present any great difficulties. You cannot grow Rhododendrons where there is lime; Clematis is happier if it does not have its roots (the soil over them, of course) in full sun, but these are the exceptions everyone learns early. There is a difference though in growing shrubs and growing them well. Take it as a general rule that the more you give, the more you receive. It tells you in *Ecclesiastes* to 'cast thy bread upon the waters: for thou shalt find it after many days' also 'give a portion to seven and also to eight, for thou knowest not what evil shall be on the earth'. I'm not sure that doing good for the sake of what you'll get out of it is the best philosophy, but it is sound gardening, and the finest shrubs grow where they have been sited thoughtfully, given suitable soil, fed well and have had care when it was needed.

It is my own view that siting – putting them in the most suitable positions – is the first important step. This is not theory: I have learned the hard way. There are two aspects to the siting of shrubs: you have to please the plants and you have to please yourself. The plants first.

Leaving the question of soil for the moment, shrubs, in common with other plants, do not thrive in strong, or cold or drying winds. Some stand them better than others. If you live by or near the sea you will find that Tamarisk, Veronica, Escallonia, Olearia will stand a good deal of pushing about, and if your garden is really troubled by high winds from the sea those, singly or mixed, will make a fine windbreak behind which you can grow less tolerant subjects. Even with those mentioned you

18

may find it advisable to have them on the leeward side of some wooden fencing till they get going strongly.

Inland, the problem is not quite the same. Obviously a south-westerly aspect is not the happiest in a country where three gales out of four come from that compass point. But the small garden does not offer all the choice we would like, and compromise is necessary. Again, shelter belts, fencing or tough shrubs, are the answer. If it is a shrub hedge you fancy to take the brunt of the wind nothing is better than a row of the despised Victorian Laurel – and a very handsome hedge it makes with its strong glossy, dark green leaves. This is the cherry Laurel, *Prunus laurocerasus*, but the Portugal laurel, *P. lusitanica*, with smaller leaves and pretty flowers and berries is nearly as good. But there is plenty of choice if you remember that to get shelter from wind you should plant strong evergreens. So you can use Cypress or *Lonicera nitida* or *Berberis* or like Evelyn grow a thick hedge of Holly. That hedge was ruined by Peter the Great, who occupied Evelyn's house when he was studying at Deptford dockyard: he used to get his servants to bowl him *through* it in a wheelbarrow! If you do not like evergreens use Oak or Beech, for they hold to their dead leaves through the winter and so give almost as good protection as shrubs that keep their foliage.

A strong south-westerly will batter a good shrub cruelly, but the bitter, dry, north to east winds we get for weeks together in spring do as much or even more damage, especially to anything newly planted. A windbreak hedge may again be the answer though you can often make do, like the shepherd at lambing time, with a few hurdles or a section or two of wooden fence. Since the drying winds are not as persistent as the prevailing ones, the shelter can be removed for most of the year.

If you do not like what you choose to plant for a windbreak it does not really matter. It's not like marriage where you have to (or should!) stick to what you get for the rest of your life. That's one of the nice things about gardening – you can have a change any time.

Hardy shrubs are not damaged by frost. That is what the title indicates. But there are degrees of hardiness and there is a lot of variation in the intensity of frost. My garden, which is on the cold side in winter, I regard as something like halfway between the warm south and the very cold north. In it my Fuchsias will grow and survive the winter, but there has never been a year since they were planted when frosts have failed to cut them down to ground level. In Cornwall frosts hardly ever affect them: the Fuchsia hedges remain hedges; in many parts of the north they are killed off completely in winter if they remain outside. We have so many climates in this country: it complicates gardening rather, for it means that there are no firm rules like 'the laws of the Medes and Persians which altereth not'. On the other hand it's every man for himself and you don't know what you can do till you try. Offhand I cannot think of any shrub which is improved by frost, and the frosts which come after a long mild spell that has set the sap moving can be deadly. So in planting look for places that offer some protection from the hardest frosts. There are nearly as many micro-climates (I *think* that is the right word!) in the garden as there are in the country as a whole. They are worth seeking out. The cold air that is going to drop to freezing point tends to move downwards (the fruit farmer says frost 'flows' downhill). That means the top of a sloping garden is warmer than it is under the hedge, fence or wall at the bottom. Down there is the 'frost pocket' and down there you may well look at the lovely Magnolia you planted and wonder why the opening buds have turned a nasty brown colour.

In the small or medium-sized garden you must grow *something*. Yes, indeed, put a bed or border of late flowers there; or, better still, your lawns. Of all plants I think grass suffers least and recovers most quickly from very low temperatures.

There is one other important point to think of when choosing a site for your shrubs and that is what point of the compass they will face. Again this is something I have learned the hard way. My house faces south and west. A very good aspect because we collect all the sunshine there is going. But about siting, just to give two examples; at the bottom of the garden someone planted a Laburnum many years ago close to the boundary wall. It looks very gay when it is in full bloom in May or June. But the side facing the house faces east – a cool aspect – the far side of the tree, the west side hanging over the road has so much more blossom on it than we see, you would not think it was the same tree. There are other shrubs and trees on that boundary and it is the same story all along. Similarly, by the south boundary wall there is an old Cherry tree that every year is laden with double white flowers. But the inside is the north side of the tree; to see what a magnificent sight it is we must go into the road. Not very satisfactory!

You would think the north fence at least would make up for all but no! My predecessors planted a row of Poplars there. Very lovely trees they are I admit with their golden yellow leaves trembling (because their wood was used for the Cross, someone told me) all summer long but they grow too fast and send their roots too wide. Now if *they* had been by the south wall and if the Cherries and Scarlet Hawthorn and Laburnum had been in their place we should have lots more shrub colour. I could move them, I agree, but alas, I approach the age when moving big strongly-rooted trees and shrubs is no longer a bit of fun! The grasshopper has not exactly become a burden but I weigh him up with a wary eye!

To return to the original bit of advice. Summed up it means you must remember that a large shrub will probably flower much more freely on the sunny side than on the shady side. So try to have the sunny side where it will most often be seen.

This brings us to the very important subject of plans, design (roughly the same) and layout, which means where the various plants are to go.

Going back to the siting problem, it is obviously better to have your shrub garden, if you intend it to be a separate department, on the north or east side of your plot. On a rectangular plot you could have it, very roughly, in a triangle in the north-east corner. In fact, I regard that as the ideal place, though it will probably be difficult to arrange a layout there in any except completely new gardens. In established gardens we have to compromise, and often some new plan must be married to what is already in place.

Always, when considering planning problems, one is influenced by one's own garden. Many years ago in my half-acre trees were planted that no doubt were handsome young saplings. But the young Oak tree on the north side is now a very vigorous adult, and even if I wanted to I don't see how I could fell it or move it. And there are two fine Copper Beeches that are very handsome indeed. I could not move them and I'd hate to chop them down. I like them. But they are much too big for the garden.

Fitting in the odd shrub here and there is easy enough. But planning or replanning a garden or a part of a garden for shrubs may not be. It depends on so many factors: size and climate – and, of course, what you want. Anybody can order ten or twenty pounds' worth and just shove them in. If they are like Reginald Arkell's Gladys's Sweet Peas it will be a case of 'Golly, how they grow!' On the other hand, they may not. The design of a garden is really work for a trained expert. But some of the experts charge a lot of money (they are worth it, I'm sure) and many people would prefer to put that into more or better shrubs, and anyhow, basically, the elements of the art are simple. You want to plan with taste; you have to visualise something near what the mature effect will be: you must try to avoid clashes of size – not growing a 6-inch Rhododendron against a 6-foot one, to give an extreme example; you must avoid clashing colours – keep soft pink flowers away from fiery Magentas; small shrubs must not be hidden by tall ones, the view of your shrub garden must be pleasing from most parts, whether house or the rest of the garden, yet all must not be on view; you want a few surprises, a colourful plant to greet you unexpectedly as you go round a corner.

Whether you plant a few ornamental trees as a background, a Maple that will be brilliant in leaf, a Copper Beech, a Weeping Willow, will depend on your personal wishes, and to some extent on the size of the ground. Generally speaking the big trees are not for the small gardens: if you really want them, plant them, but be prepared to remove them when they grow so large that they throw everything else out of proportion. Also big trees, like big dogs, are hungry brutes, and their roots wander far and wide with the exploratory enthusiasm of a Columbus.

As to the size of the shrubs, roughly speaking they will graduate from tall at the back to dwarf at the front, yet do not make this a very rigid rule. Only the most sergeant-majorish type of mind will insist on a complete even slope from rear to front: I don't mean that sergeant-majors aren't nice chaps, but discipline is not for shrubs! What the poet called a sweet disorder in the dress is more pleasant to the view; a rise and fall, almost in waves. And never, never, plant in straight even rows as if you were putting in a plantation of Larches. I will modify that: I am a great believer in every gardener doing not what the rule book says but entirely what he wants. So have straight rows if you *like* them. Otherwise not!

It again comes to the size of the plot and what species you want. In a large garden where you want only your own special favourites you can go in for grouping: six Lilacs here, a couple of Magnolias there and a collection of Berberis somewhere else, though there is nothing against splitting them up if you prefer it that way.

I think a small area is perhaps more difficult because you have to harmonise not the same shrubs but single specimens of all shapes, sizes and colours. Where there is a planting of any size it is wise to start off with a plan drawn on paper. The garden designer will make out a very artistic-looking map, but one that shows the shape of the garden, to scale if possible, and some shilling-sized circles, one to represent each bush, will do just as well. Try various things in different places, shift them around until you have what you feel is the best arrangement, and even then be prepared to change and alter when you come to plant.

Remember that even your planting need not be final. When the time comes for you to look on your work and contemplate, don't be too proud to put right any mistakes. What you have planted you do not want to dig up again, but young shrubs will not suffer overmuch from a careful transplanting.

Now heed the gipsy's warning! You must remember that what you put in, thinking you've not got much for all that money, will in a few years grow into a very bonny thing that spreads faster than a fat woman who lives entirely on potatoes and chocolates. For instance, you plant three Lilac trees and they look such miserable little creatures that you want to place them only a foot apart if only to prevent their dying of loneliness. But if you do you will have to find room elsewhere for a couple of them in a few years' time. The thickly planted shrub garden becomes an impenetrable jungle very quickly. All right for a windbreak perhaps (though even then they get bare at the base in no time) but you don't see the flowers for the trees and they have a struggle for the nutrients in the soil.

Good nursery catalogues usually give the expected ultimate sizes, and these vary a lot, naturally. Plan with these sizes in mind. You need not be ruled rigidly by them for you can always prune and trim back the too hearty spreaders, but the proportions given should be considered.

The one way you can get the quick results that close planting gives (you hope) is to plant more than will finally be required and remove some as the space becomes filled. The drawback is that it is an expensive method; also most dedicated gardeners hate throwing something good away and when removal time comes you have an unhappy man wandering about looking for a space for a good shrub he has been forced to dig up.

Chapter 3: SOIL

As a rule shrubs grow well in most average soils. There are some that do not thrive where lime is present; there are others that will die if you plant them in lime soils. Rhododendrons are the best-known examples of this intolerance, but Magnolias, Camellias, and most of the Heather family are others, and there are many more, less well known, less often grown, that lime will poison.

I am gardener rather than plant-biologist but I understand the reason is not that lime actually poisons them but that its action on the soil locks up elements without which they cannot thrive. To some extent this lime-dislike has been conquered by the use of a substance called Sequestrene with which you can water the roots of, say, Rhododendrons when they are planted in inhospitable soils. This may be fine. I hope it is but I have never had to use it, for my garden soil is naturally so acid that Rhododendrons grow in it as easily as Mustard and Cress. This gives me the best of two worlds, for anything that needs lime can have it – out of a bag. Don't envy me. Anyone who gardens on a cold Welsh hillside can do with all the advantages he can get – though fine scenery is a consolation when you look at the frost-blackened blossoms on the Magnolia!

There are some shrubs that do their best in lime soil; Clematis are one, they thrive on it; Lilacs appreciate it, also Buddleias, and you may take it that any shrub which in more usual form is grown for stone fruit positively must have lime to form healthy seed-protecting stones. That brings in the Cherries, Almonds, Peaches, Plums, the Purple Plums mainly and a Purple-leafed Sloe, *Prunus spinosa purpurea*, and Laurels.

In between the shrubs that dislike lime and those that must have it to keep them healthy there is the crowd of others that seem not to care much (how easily we talk of plants as if they were human!) one way or the other.

When an area or a garden has been planted with shrubs the soil will not get much cultivation. There, of course, lies a lot of their attraction. Plant them and forget them. You may hoe a little but not if you underplant; prune a little, mulch or give a little fertiliser. So it is a good thing to prepare the soil as thoroughly as you can before the shrubs go in. It may be all they will get in their lifetime. In earlier days the ground might have been trenched or double-trenched, which means digging two spits deep or even three spits deep. Gardeners really did that once as a matter of course or if they would not or could not there was always some jobbing gardener who would do the task for the matter of a few shillings. Some experts have cast a doubt on whether all the trouble was worth it; I think it was. I once saw a large area of garden that had been very deeply dug indeed – to three feet I should think – not in the interests of the garden but because the gardener was hunting for a buried pipe. The plants that were later planted on that bit of ground were incredibly good and immeasurably better than in any other part of the garden.

But these days most of us are content with a good, single spade (or fork) depth of digging and as a rule it suffices well enough. With this digging should go the addition of material that will enrich the soil, and it must be mixed in as thoroughly as possible. The best soil improver still is farmyard manure. That is a memory now for most gardeners, but compost is almost as good. Sometimes compost is short of nitrogen, so a little nitro chalk can be added as well. Other useful materials are seaweed, which is probably as good as farm manure, leafmould, hop manure. There are some good fertilisers that come from the rotted-down waste of certain industries; hop manure is one of these; others are hoof-and-horn and shoddy, which I believe is rotted waste from the woollen mills. It is worth noting that anything that once was part of living matter will rot down and enrich soil. The rate of rotting does vary though, crumpled newspaper rots fairly quickly but coconut fibre seems to last indefinitely and the stuffing of an old spring mattress which I buried once had to be buried deeply and hardly yielded quick results. The contents of a discarded feather bed was rather better and was soon part of the soil. Peat is more useful to improve the texture of soil than as plant food. To dig in large quantities all over a garden would be very expensive, but it can be used in the planting sites of certain shrubs, especially those that won't grow in lime soils.

Bonfire ash is useful on all soils, adding a number of minerals – potash in particular. But it is better to rot waste into compost than to burn it in a bonfire, so the garden bonfire, once looked on as a regular autumn task (some gardeners burned their leaves: a horticultural crime if ever there was one!) is better saved for only the most intractable materials like tree stumps and old motor tyres!

If you do have a bonfire *and* you have clay try to burn as much clay as you can on it. Burned clay is splendid stuff, and there is no soil which will not benefit from it.

That brings me gently to the subject of clay, and it is a subject I am familiar with because I cannot dig deeply anywhere in my garden without finding lots of it, yellow, as heavy as lead and either brick hard or as sticky as Christmas pudding. But in clay are nearly all the nutrients plants need, and soil based on clay is always fertile. The trouble is how to make these nutrients available to the plants. Well, the clay must be broken up as far as possible and other materials, such as grit, ashes, manure, compost, leaves, mixed with it. Do not try to dig up and improve all the clay in a garden in one big campaign. That way lies heartbreak. Attack a small piece at a time and in the end you will win. The two things that will give most assistance in breaking down clay are frost and lime. So try to turn the stuff in autumn and on genial winter days and leave it in large rough lumps. Do not try to break it. Together the frost and lime will turn it to a good crumbly texture by spring, and then the manures you give it will tame it to a loam that will easily be warmed by the sun and become neither sticky nor hard.

What if you have a hard stratum of clay too deep down to work? In that case do not worry overmuch. Roots themselves will do a lot to break up obstinate soils. The older gardeners used to say you could not expect roots to penetrate a hard pan of clay. That was rubbish. Roots will penetrate *anything*, given time enough. My lovely old horse chestnut tree, so beautiful in spring when it was covered with pink blossom, sent its roots down twelve feet (at least) and so completely filled a drain that the tree had to be cut down. After all nature planted many a fine forest on land that had not been cultivated at all, and most of them thrived mightily. The roots of your shrubs may take longer to get through clay than they would to penetrate a light porous soil, but they will do it in time.

Chapter 4: PLANTING

'To every thing there is a season and a time to every purpose under heaven . . . a time to plant and a time to pluck up that which is planted.'

How difficult it is to say anything that has not already been said – and said better.

One of the youngsters once remarked that *Ecclesiastes* was out of date. You can plant out of containers now and so any time is a time to plant. But that is a sort of repotting: the planting had already been done, in the container, *in its season*.

Planting time extends from October to March, give or take a week or two. In that period the shrubs may be planted any time the soil and the weather are suitable. That means that *most* planting will be carried out mainly in October and early November, or in March. The sooner the plant goes to its new home before it starts to grow, the better. It has longer to settle down and roots, never completely dormant, will have longer to make themselves at home. But roots do not like cold and wet any more than we do, so a good general rule is to plant in autumn on light, warm soils and in spring on heavy ones. This is a counsel of perfection, of course; the man or woman who has to garden at weekends or in holidays must get things in when he or she can. As a rule it does not make any difference, though over the years I have lost an odd rose bush now and again after an autumn planting.

Evergreens must be taken separately and they benefit from more careful treatment. In winter their roots are not active enough to supply the necessary plant foods to keep leaves healthy.

This can result in leaf dropping and if new leaves do not come along quickly the plant will die. So it is better not to plant in winter. There are robust customers like the Hypericums it seems impossible to kill, but it is always the choice specimens you paid a fortune for that, like the (Victorian) good, die young. The best times to plant evergreens are September–October and April–May. Probably the first is the better, for the soil still holds the warmth of summer; roots can get to work at once and the risk of complete leaf-shedding through dryness or dry winds is almost nil. If a spell of north or east winds persists a piece of sacking as a covering would be a help, and I recommend sacking or mats, or even dry straw, over the branches in case of prolonged hard frosts. A snow covering is usually harmless though its weight can break branches.

If planting of evergreens is done in late spring more care is needed. The soil is apt to be much colder after the winter than it was in autumn, and you have to keep the roots moist without making the soil cold and wet. It is worth filling in the holes in which the trees are planted with a light gritty compost. The spring winds often blow from north or east for weeks at a time and the damp-sack technique is a great help in keeping the leaves alive until the roots can supply plenty of moisture. It pays to watch newly-planted shrubs, evergreens in particular, in their first season for signs that moisture is needed. A good watering in a dry spell, followed by a thick mulch of peat or lawn clippings, has saved many a root-dry shrub from disaster. This planting advice refers mainly to planting shrubs that have been growing in beds in the nursery. That kind of planting will be with us for a long time to come because there will always (not a word to use lightly!) be people who cannot go to the nursery to collect their own plants. But more and more of us are planting from containers nowadays and it seems obvious that the use of this method will increase. It has so many advantages. The nurseryman plants his stock in cheap containers. You can buy these, take them home and can plant when you like; if a few simple precautions are observed, at any time of the year, though sensible gardeners would avoid doing it in baking drought and would not try to do it in hard frost or when snow was on the ground. Losses should be very rare when planting from containers: evergreens in particular will be much easier to move. But the advice given for when you are using open-ground plants still holds; in particular, the need to protect from drought and cold drying winds.

The actual method of planting is virtually the same also. You hardly need telling what to do. I should imagine that planting is almost an instinct, but a little imagination helps. Only a child would open out a small hole in a hard pan of soil and cram the roots of any plant in it. The hole in which you will plant should be dish shaped and wide. It does not have to be deep. Aim at having the main stem slightly below what it was in the nursery. If it is an open-ground shrub spread the roots comfortably, cover these with some good light soil until the ground is level again and the shrub firm. If it is any size, or top-heavy, put in a stake and tie it firmly. You can do this as you spread the roots or you can do it after filling in. Some folk get worried about damaging the roots but I do not think it matters greatly. A bit of root more or less is nothing between friends. Roots, like the Hydra's head, increase in geometric progression. Cut one off and (generally) two grow in its place. I usually cut back any long old thongy roots before I plant roses, and it is well known that the check given by root pruning will often cause a non-flowering shrub to flower and a non-fruiting tree to bear fruit.

From this point the cultivation demanded by the inhabitants of your Shrub Garden will be very small. That does not mean you have to neglect them, but they can go on with very little attention and you can enjoy them without worrying about some care you ought to give them. You need not cosset them. You must be sure they are staked if they are the sort of things that blow about, but, once growing strongly, most of them are not. If they are in very light soil they may need watering during a drought, but if the soil was well prepared they should not; the roots will forage deeply for water. Here, like any other gardener, I am ruled by experience in my own garden. My soil holds water – too much rather than too little, in winter anyhow – and having to water shrubs is an almost unheard-of chore. (I have weakened and refreshed thirsty roses a few times!)

In light soils mulches are useful. In my own case this means spreading the lawn mowings at the base of shrubs where the ground is bare round them. This smothers weeds, helps to keep the moisture in the soil; probably also keeps the spores of rusts and moulds off leaves, and eventually improves the soil, both in texture and in food content.

At some time the question of ground cover will arise but again this is a job that once done can be left for many years. Again I speak from experience.

Magnolia soulangeana is best as a wall shrub in cold districts

Kerria japonica (below), the yellow Gypsy Rose, is rather stiff and formless – but full of colour

Syringa. This old-fashioned single white lilac grows quickly and easily and is
the best for scent

Chapter 5: PRUNING

Young gardeners and those new to the craft get very worried about pruning. To some people it is one of the great mysteries. But it is not a mystery because in the widest sense, that is, in nature, in thickets, and woods and small forests and primaeval forests there is never any pruning at all. Or what there is happens naturally: weak branches die, dead branches fall and in the course of time become part of the soil from whence they came.

We prune for one of two reasons: either to get more and better flowers, or to keep the bush a certain size and shape.

Taking the first reason: this is best understood by most gardeners by using the tea roses as an example. As a rule the bushes give their best blooms on new shoots. So we cut off the old ones and a thicket of young branches springs up and each gives one or more flowers. But remember the rose trees would bear good flowers if they were not pruned at all. Some rose enthusiasts like it that way. They prune not at all or very lightly and call it long pruning. In some gardens and on some soils it can be very successful.

Shrubs bear their best flowers either on branches that grew the year before or on branches that will grow this year. In the former case they can be pruned, generally quite hard, as soon as they have finished flowering. The shrub then sends out a lot of new branches and on these the flowers will blossom next year.

In the latter case the shrubs can be cut back in spring (as with the roses) and shoots will grow and bear flowers in a few months' time.

This pruning, in both cases, must be done with care, or some very ugly shapes and forms can result. The larger shrubs are the greater sufferers and are sometimes headed back cruelly, reminding one of the cold nakedness of shorn sheep. On the other hand, if you have planted something that is getting right out of hand and overshadowing and robbing everything in sight then you have to take a firm line. A willow, for instance, can grow into an enormous tree (look at the old ones on river banks). That makes them unsuitable for small gardens; pollarded back to a head, say eight feet from the ground, they can be quite handsome in their own way; if you do not like pollarded trees (bearing a head of branches from a straight bare trunk) do not plant those trees at all, and if someone else has planted them have them removed.

Often an overpowering shrub can be given a completely new start. Some of my old *Rhododendron ponticum* grow much too large in certain spots. I then cut them back almost to ground level. They look bare and ugly but send up a crop of lusty young branches and in no time at all the bushes are rounded, handsome and full of vigour again.

They have form, grace, a beauty of shape, call it what you will, and that is most important in shrubs. In fact it is almost as important as the flowers. You get form in the pyramid of a Cypress tree, a Lombardy Poplar (but don't plant these unless you have acres) in a Weeping Willow, in a Silver Birch. You do not get it, or very rarely get it, in sprawling plants like Clematis and Rambler Roses.

If you want form you keep pruning to a minimum; generally cutting out only thin weak shoots, dead ones, and too vigorous ones that spoil the shape. You won't get much form in hard-pruned Rambler Roses, but big bushes of a lot of the old-fashioned Roses growing unpruned are a joy to look at.

I have an *Azalea pontica* with yellow flowers so heavily scented that its fragrance meets you a dozen yards away on a warm spring morning. It was growing strongly when I took over the garden more than twenty years ago. I have never cut off so much as a single shoot, and the shape is perfect, even and rounded. It is a joy from the first bright flowers to the last crimson leaf and then is still a pleasant companion because the form is right.

You mostly see form at its best in the winter. Well-treated deciduous shrubs (or trees – don't look only at what is inside the garden) have each their own particular characteristics. The Birch trees have a filigree of delicate twigs, the Oak spreads strongly fanwise, the Beech is nearly as laced as the Birch but spreads more and could never be mistaken for anything but what it is. Good similes are difficult to find. This part of the book should be written by a poet. I look out of the window and the shrubs I neglect are all different, all good to look at: the tall Rugosa bush, the Lilacs, the Purple Plum, the Sweet Briar. You could not, even with the worst eyesight, mistake one for the other. They are alike only in that each has form.

Yes indeed, pruning is a very important part of shrub culture – unless and until you *must*, don't do it at all.

Chapter 6: PROPAGATION

Propagation of your own shrubs is fun. That is not quite the word, but it is near enough. It can give you great pleasures. There are some shrubs that I would not try to increase for myself. The Magnolias for instance: not exactly difficult but so slow (from layers) as to tax your patience. The majority of popular shrubs are easy, though some are easier than others. It makes the day-to-day gardening more interesting when you have a little nursery of your own coming along. Even if you should have no room for more you can always give the young plants away. I'm not sure it is true that it is more blessed to give than to receive – it all depends, as our roadman said, whether it's a blow or a few bob – but a feeling that you are generous is quite good for you.

The only drawback to growing your own shrubs is that it *can* be slow. A rooted cutting or a seedling may take a few years to reach planting-out size. So I do not think we shall put the nurseries out of business.

There are three common methods of propagation. The most obvious is by sowing seeds; the next is from cuttings, then layers. These are the most used by amateurs. Then there is division; some shrubs send out suckers which are new plants growing on the parent roots. These can be detached and will make new shrubs. The professional gardeners use the specialised techniques of budding and grafting for hardwood trees. These are not necessarily difficult methods but you do have to learn how they are done, and you have to practise them to become really good at them. There are still a few other ways of increasing your stocks,

like air propagation and inarching but a full treatise on propaga-
tions needs a volume* not a chapter, and there really is not the
time to do everything.

Sowing seeds seems the most natural way to increase any
plant, and it is the easiest if you can get the seeds. Sometimes you
cannot, and sometimes when you do get them they take a weary
time a-growing. I don't think rose seeds germinate until they
have lain in the soil for a year; this is called stratification. You
can stratify them by storing them in sand. I sow them straight off
and wait, though I put in only the occasional few from something
like *Rosa moyesii*. Generally, you get something inferior to the
parent plant. It is a gamble. You may obtain an improved strain,
but don't expect it.

In a garden where many shrubs and trees grow, self-sown
seedlings come up all over the place. They are mainly the more
common shrubs, though they are none the worse for that; but
they are not always easy to dispose of unless you know some
young gardener who is stocking-up his brand-new bit of earth.
Occasionally I get something a little out of the ordinary: the
little group of Pines and Spruce in the far corner give me a few
seedlings here and there: and there are quite a few self-sown
Rhododendrons about. Hollies, from my one berrying tree,
come up everywhere. I can generally find a few Laburnums,
Mahonias, Flowering Currants, Daphnes (the green-flowered
D. laureola or Spurge Laurel), Brooms, and masses of little bushes
of Ling (*Calluna*). Homes can usually be found for these, but the
Geans (Wild Cherries), Ash, Oak, Willow, Thorn, Mountain
Ash and Hazel are not so easy. My friends with small plots view
them with suspicion and (in the garden) I do hate throwing
anything away. My wife, luckily, feels no such tenderness, and
will put on the rubbish heap any sapling that grows where it
should not grow, but I feel like a reluctant executioner as I turn
down my thumb!

Propagation is best carried on in a small area set aside for the

* I wrote one years ago: *Gardening on a Shoestring:* long out of print but probably still
available at some libraries.

purpose. Seedlings and cuttings can be grown in it and transplanted in the fullness of time to where they are needed. But if you share my reluctance to dispose of surplus plants do not over-propagate.

Cuttings are shoots that you take off the parent shrub. They root most easily when taken off where they grow on a branch. You trim the thick end – called heels – and insert them in a narrow trench, preferably on sand or gritty soil. As a rule they will make a healthy root system in about a year. If the ends are dipped in a hormone rooting powder, which can be bought at any garden shop, they will form roots more quickly and more certainly. But gardeners put in cuttings ('slips' means the same thing by the way) for thousands of years before rooting powders were available, so, though helpful, they are not essential.

The best shrubs for growing from cuttings are what are called soft-woods. A complete list is hardly possible but almost anything is worth a try. Perhaps Roses are the most worthwhile. Success with these is very variable. In some gardens they root with difficulty; in others they are grown *only* on their own roots and very successfully too. William Robinson, a giant of a gardener in Victorian times, would have them that way or not at all.

'The first care should be to get plants on their own roots about as strong as those worked,' (he meant budded) 'and it is not difficult to do this with a little patience.'

So he wrote in *The English Flower Garden* and since he did know what he was talking about and practised what he preached his advice is worth quoting.

'The best time to make cuttings of the half-ripened wood is in September, or, in warm valleys, a little later. Our cuttings are usually about 10 inches long and often with a heel, and are inserted for the greater part of their length in the freest sandy loam in the place . . . For the Teas and Chinas the best soil is a free sandy loam in which the roots can find all they need.'

Roses for nothing! Lots and lots of Roses for nothing – if you can get the cuttings! With prices what they are it's quite a thought.

If certain shrubs do not grow easily from cuttings it is probably because the wood is rather hard and this kind roots so slowly that the cutting dies of starvation before it has roots to feed it. In that case you practise layering. It means that you do not take it from its parent until it *has* formed roots. Rhododendrons and Magnolias are of this kind. Take a low branch, cut out a tiny nick (wedge) below a bud, peg it at that spot to the ground and cover with a small mound of good light soil. Each layer will take about two years to build up a good root system. Then it can be cut off and planted elsewhere. Old bushes of Rhododendrons will often root branches on their own and the first I ever grew were rooted branches I found on ancient noble bushes that had probably been growing half a century.

About the easiest method of all is division but there is a limited number of shrubs with which this can be done and some of them can be a nuisance in the garden. They sucker freely and where you put in one plant there are, after a few years, a group. The outer stems of a group can be dug up and started off as new plants. Gipsy Rose (*Kerria japonica*) is a pleasant example. Others can often become spreading terrors. Snowberry (*Symphoricarpus*) will wander far and wide and can get right out of control. Common Lilac also can be more of a pest than a pleasure and unfortunately the nurseries have sometimes used this as a stock on which to graft choice varieties. The result can be a very handsome Lilac in the centre surrounded (like the Old Woman Who Lived in a Shoe) by a host of less decorative subjects.

Some suckers are easy to control: Lilac is not and getting rid of unwanted suckers is a problem, especially as new ones are always apt to spring from damaged roots. So digging them out is often not much help – yet what else *can* you do?

There is no definite list as to what will or will not sucker, so it pays to keep a watch. My *Viburnum fragrans* sent up one lovely shoot that made a very fine new plant, and often a choice shrub will send a new shoot up from ground level and it may root and if it does there is an extra shrub all for nothing. It can happen anywhere: I have known a fruit tree behave so, and my old Hugh

Dickson Rose made such a tangle at ground level that I was able to dig it up, split it into a dozen new plants and give quite a lot away.

Those are the easiest methods of propagation. Air layering consists of 'nicking' a stem, wrapping it in damp moss, which must be kept damp, wrapping the moss in a cellophane bandage and detaching when roots form in the moss. Easy, actually, but not usual and not, I think, too successful with hard-wooded shrubs.

Inarching is to some extent a specialist's method used on shrubs which present difficulties when the more conventional methods are used. It consists of uniting the stem of a shrub to the stem of a 'parent' stock, cutting the bark off where the surfaces meet, bandaging them there and leaving them until they join. More interesting than useful to the amateur, though in nature you often – or should that be 'occasionally' – find it happen. I think this method is used with Vines, Oranges and Lemons, but I have no wide experience of it.

This leaves us with budding and grafting. These, like inarching, depend on the fact that an inner layer of bark, the cambium layer of a plant, will unite with the cambium layer on another of the same species.

I don't think any gardener learns to bud and graft from a text-book or by reading about the methods in books. They are learned by practice. Sometimes they seem incredibly difficult and you may get one failure after another, but once you acquire the skill you can have a hundred per cent success.

For anyone interested here are brief précis of both methods.

Budding is practised occasionally in tree fruits but most commonly with hybrid tea roses.

As a stock, briars are used and they should be prepared from seeds or cuttings, a year before they are needed. The budding of Roses is carried out from June to September.

The actual budding is done in this way: Buds of the rose are cut out of the stem with a tiny ellipse of the stem. Out of this you carefully pull the bit of wood, leaving the bark and the bud. On the stock a T-shaped cut is made. You slip the shield of bark holding the bud into the cut, trim off the bit of bark that protrudes at the top, bind with raffia (I learned to do it with raffia; I don't know what they use now) and really that's the lot. With luck the cambium layers grow together, the branch of the briar is cut back to the bud in March, the bud carries on from there and becomes a new rose bush.

I have purposely simplified that. This is not a book on propagation, but there is enough to help anyone who wants to bud roses, or anything else, to get started. I knew less when I did my first budding and I grew lots of new bushes and a lot of standard Roses – which were far too costly for me to buy – and even a few Weeping Standards by budding ramblers on tall standard single-stem stocks I gathered (painfully!) from thickets and hedges.

Grafting is the same as budding in principle but now you unite stems of the desired variety (apples or pears or what you will) to a stock, perhaps the wild type, that makes a strong root system.

There are many methods of grafting and a volume on propagation will give you the complete list and discuss the advantages and disadvantages of each.

Here, purely for your interest, and to help you should you care to try, I will again simplify to the point of what my Candid Friend calls (no offence!) Idiot's Delight, and I will take one method only called Crown Grafting.

You have an ancient and useless apple tree, which is strong and vigorous but bears fruit with the horrible taste of cotton wool flavoured with cider vinegar.

Grafting is done in spring when the sap is moving. Select shoots of the variety you want to grow, remove them from the tree and heel them in somewhere. This is so that they will not be too advanced in growth at grafting time. These are called scions. In early spring, say late March, cut the old apple tree off a foot or two from the ground. Cut it horizontally. Two or three scions are usually grown on each stock. The scions are prepared by cutting them at a very acute angle with a long sloping cut. The bark at the side of the stock is slit to the wood and the bark gently lifted. Into each slit a scion is inserted, the cut surface inwards. You bandage this up with a wad of clay. Thus we have, supposing three scions are used, a stump from the top of which three small branches stick upwards at a slight angle. These will grow into your new tree, which in due course will bear enormous crops of delicious juicy apples. We hope so!

Easy, isn't it? Well yes, and no. It's like everything else – you live and learn. Once any cottager in apple country – Hereford-shire or Worcestershire say, could graft in his sleep. Nowadays he goes seawards at week-ends in his Mini or his Bentley, and he buys his apple trees from the nursery. But if you *can* graft and *do* graft you can get a great spiritual satisfaction (I don't want to sound too elevated!) out of doing it. If you would learn more of the theory get a book on the subject, like my *Gardening on a Shoestring*, or, a much more exhaustive volume than mine, *The Propagation of Plants* by G. J. King (Hutchinson). These should be obtainable at libraries.

Now, for your pleasure and delight, the lunatic fringe. Years ago a countryman told me that if you took cuttings, split the end and inserted a grain of wheat they would root more easily. I have not experimented enough with this – trying with and without and comparing results – to be able to say if the trick is worth while but it is well known that layers that are split at the point where roots are to form root better if something is done to hold the split open.

And this is from my book: 'An interesting method of raising apple trees came to light in a letter to *The Countryman*. A correspondent, Mr H. A. Brader of Lincoln, found an account of it in a note on the flyleaf of a dictionary published in 1781. "The process is to take the shoots from the choicest sorts, insert them in a potatoe and plunge both into the ground, leaving but an inch or two of the shoot above the surface. The Potatoe nourishes the shoot while it pushes out its roots, and the shoot gradually grows up and becomes a beautiful tree bearing the best fruit."

'This is said to have been used to raise orchards in Bohemia.'

It sounds a typical countryman's trick, but I do not think I ever got around to trying it.

Here is a bit more lore on propagation.

'For to graffe the Rose, that his leaves shall keep all the year green, some do take and cleave the holly, and do graffe in a red or white Rose-bud; and then put clay and mosse to him and let him grow. And some put the Rose-bud into a slit of the bark and so put clay and mosse, and bind him featly therein and let him grow and he shall carry his leaf all the year.' – *The Countryman's Recreation* (1654).

Gerard, as you might expect, had something to say on the subject:

'The Yellow Rose which (as divers do report) was by Art so coloured, and altered from his first estate, by grafting a wilde Rose upon a Broome-stalk, whereby (say they) it doth not only change his colour, but his smell and force.' Even Gerard did not believe that.

Finally, and perhaps best of all, a bit of advice from Robert Salle who in the fifteenth century was an authority (so they say) on grafting.

'Yf thou wilt make thyn apples reede, take the graffe of an appel tree And graffe hit on a stok of elme or aldyr and hit shall ber' reede apples.'

Also: 'Make an hole wt a wymbell in a tree and what colour thu wilt distempre hit with water and put it in at the hole and the fruit shal be of the same colour.'

Well, as our roadman said when they put pepper in his beer, *I'll try anything once*. But I don't think I shall bother with that one!

Chapter 7: THE SHRUBS

ACER I am not making a very good start, for Acer is the Latin name of Maple and our most familiar Maple is the Sycamore and that can quickly grow into a very large tree. But there are some species that are small enough and handsome enough to deserve a place in any garden, not for their flowers but for the brilliance of the scarlet leaves. The best is *Acer palmatum atropurpureum*, one of the Japanese Maples. It is as brilliant a coloured shrub as you can find and does not grow too large, in fact can be cut back if it happens to overspread itself, and shoots out well and renews itself when it is pruned. While all species of Acer are hardy the leaves are susceptible to frost damage – Sycamores will often suffer this way when there are late spring frosts – but if the frosted shoots are cut off they soon renew themselves. All the Maples are said to dislike windy situations.

There are many other ornamental Maples, some large, some small, and while the Scarlet Maple or Japanese Maple, already mentioned, is undoubtedly the best for the small garden there are other very pretty ones with ornamental leaves. But it is a genus of which to be wary. There are at least some fifty species available at one nursery or another so it is a family in which you should shop around before deciding on, not so much what you like as what you have room for. There are lots of species of *A. palmatum*, mostly with a formidable string of names. *A. linearilobum atropurpureum* has finely divided red leaves, and there are others with golden leaves or variegated ones. The most useful of these in shrub size are *A. negundo* and its varieties. Most people have heard of the North American ones that colour so richly in autumn and more people have heard of Maple Syrup and Maple Sugar. Our own species yield a similar sweet sap, and John Evelyn said of our own Sycamore (not a true native) that 'the sap is sweet and wholesome, and in a short time yields sufficient quantity to brew with, so as with one bushel of malt is made as good ale as four bushels with ordinary water.'

AESCULUS The Horse Chestnut is definitely not for gardens. I, who say so, know it for I had to have one cut down because the roots had invaded some drains. Lovely though it is in spring, and loved as it is by small boys in autumn for its conkers, it has an alarming spread and the matted roots, as tangled and thick as a wire pan-scrubber (and nearly as tough) wander like Puck, everywhere, and nearly as swiftly!

But there is one species that is moderate in size which makes a very lovely shrub. It is *Aesculus parviflora*, a spreading bush some eight feet high and as much through. It bears in summer an abundance of white flowers with red anthers which make them appear pink. If it spreads beyond its allotted area it can be cut back. There is no common name so far as I know; indeed, though very easy and not a bit rare or difficult or tender, it is not a commonly grown shrub so can be strongly recommended to anyone wanting a change from the usual favourites. An established plant produces lots of rooted offsets so propagation is simple and spare plants always available for your visitors who have never heard of the Tenth Commandment.

The name Aesculus is from *esca*, food, and belonged, according to Pliny, to a species of Oak valued for its acorns. The switch to the Horse Chestnut seems to have been one of those errors of confusion made because the fruit resembles the edible Sweet Chestnut. It certainly is not fit food for humans, though there is a record in the *Gardeners' Chronicle* in 1843 that sheep find them nourishing, and it gives an account of their being collected in the Geneva area and used, crushed, for fattening sheep. 'Hungry sheep surely,' but it adds 'the Geneva mutton is noted for being as highly flavoured as any in England or Wales.'

The common name arose because the Chestnuts were used, said

Evelyn, 'from its curing horses broken-winded and other cattle of coughs.'

AMPELOPSIS This is not usually thought of as a shrub but it is one and a very stout shrub it can become. I don't know how large it can grow but I have a couple of specimens with trunks a good few inches through at ground level. I have never seen any species growing on flat ground – all of them are natural climbers – but presumably it would sprawl far and wide until it found something up which it could climb.

The common name is Virginia Creeper and all are grown for the brilliance of their coloured leaves in autumn.

Unfortunately the names of the various species have been altered so many times that any gardener with a horror of Latin titles could so easily get lost. I don't know if any of the family have been left under *Ampelopsis* but some are *Parthenocissus* and some are *Vitis* (the Grape Vine) and once it was even *Hedera*, which is Ivy.

It would be pedantic to try to be absolutely accurate in a book of this kind so I will use the familiar names, and, for the better-informed, guide them from the accurate to the familiar by cross-reference. There are twenty or so species you may grow but the two most favoured are the self-supporting one that climbs on walls in the same way as Ivy does, with leaves somewhat similar in shape; and the one with five lobed leaves (Horse Chestnut style) that climbs by means of tendrils.

They are pleasant climbing shrubs at any time but the glory of both is the marvellous autumn colour. They grow well in any soil and in the driest of summers never appear to suffer from drought. Most gardeners neglect their Virginia Creepers but they deserve a mulch of manure or compost from time to time and a handful of general fertiliser sprinkled around in spring would not come amiss.

The best of the wall clinging species is *A. veitchii*, which is sometimes called *A. inconstans*, other times *Vitis inconstans*. If you want larger leaves plant *A. coignetiae* (or *Vitis coignetiae*).

Ampelopsis quinquefolia has five distinct spearhead-shaped leaflets. Oh dear, my conscience is at me again! If you can't find that name in your catalogue or at the nursery try *Vitis quinquefolia*, which is not accurate, or *Parthenocissus quinquefolia*, which is correct at the moment.

It climbs by twining so needs some support to hold on to. It is good for walls or porches and is really grand on an old tree. Some shoots on one of my own plants which clambers up a porch have found their way to a Mountain Ash a few yards away and since the Mountain Ash is also gay in autumn they are a jolly couple.

But there is a snag. These Virginia Creepers colour earliest and best in full exposure, so give of their richest shades on south and west walls. But we all know what happens to autumn leaves: they fall. And our south-west gales in autumn do these climbers no good at all. An early September gale can strip them. So if you can find a little shelter yet still plenty of sun your care, like virtue, will bring its own reward.

On a corner of my conservatory greenhouse one of my *A. veitchii* has found a little crack and has come in out of the wind and the rain. It spreads over the wall – I pull it off annually or it would outgrow its welcome – and long thin stems of it droop down gracefully as well. The leaves stay till Christmas or later but, curiously, do not colour nearly as richly as they do outside.

Parthenocissus is from *parthenos*, a virgin, and *Kissos*, ivy. ' 'Tis called the Virgin Vine because . . . 'tis a Maid and has hitherto brought forth nothing.'

ARTIMESIA This is a dwarf shrub with strongly scented, feathery leaves. It is a relation of the herb Wormwood, which is a herbaceous plant, *Artimesia absinthium*, Wormwood, is used to flavour absinthe; *A. abrotanum* is almost as strongly flavoured, certainly too strong even for the terrible salt beef of the Middle Ages. But dried and put amongst linen it would – still will, presumably – keep away clothes moths and they say even fleas flinch from it.

A. abrotanum has a number of common names. Southernwood because it is a Mediterranean plant, though it is perfectly hardy, was regarded as the Wormwood of the South. It was called Old

Man because a wash made from its leaves gave old men what they so often lack: a fresh head of hair – or so they say! Lad's Love was used because the sweetly scented leaves were put in the posies the boys gave their sweethearts.

This little shrub will grow practically anywhere, in any soil. It gets up to about two feet in a season or at most two, and it is a good plan then to cut it down when it will spring up, freshly grey-green from the base.

AZALEA I have decided to treat Azalea separately from Rhododendron because in most gardener's minds and in their gardens they *are* separate. Up to a few years ago they were thought to be different, cousins as it were; but they have become brothers and sisters. The botanists say there is no real difference between them and now they are all included under the Latin generic name of *Rhododendron* which comes from 'Rose'.

Just for your amusement there is only one plant in this country, perhaps anywhere, that is truly entitled to the name Azalea. It is a very rare wild plant that grows in the Highlands and to make the amusement really hilarious the name has been changed to *Loiseleuria procumbens*! The Rev. Keble Martin has illustrated it in his gem of a wild flower book: *The Concise British Flora in Colour*, so he must have seen it. I have not.

But I'm thankful my interest is gardening and not botany.

When I started gardening most people thought that Azaleas were the leaf-losing shrubs and Rhododendrons were the evergreens. But there are evergreen Azaleas and leaf-losing Rhododendrons. Again some catalogues separate the two groups and some class them together as *Rhododendron*. And then there are hybrids between the two.

Even Frederick Street, who is so familiar with them he can address them by their first names, has written separate books (very good ones, too) on Rhododendrons and Azaleas, though of course not because he does not know who and what they are.

There are so many in cultivation now, species, sub-species, hybrids, crosses between one and another, that literally we are faced with thousands of shrubs from which to choose. They are, in spite of their aristocratic beauty, a mighty family wherein none (or few) know who their parents were. Very disreputable really.

But they don't care, so why should we.

The only thing is that it would surely be a good plan to take a very hard look at this multitude and throw some of the least worthy overboard. I open the catalogue of one of the best of our nurseries and find they stock (or offer!) about 24 pages with some 20 or more to the page. They can't *all* be so different from each other. I find myself inclined to choose as women are said to choose racehorses – with a pin. But the pin method with horses is a gamble, whereas with Azaleas or Rhododendrons you would be very unlucky to pick a loser.

The main catalogue divisions, unless you want to be very pedantic, are six. They are:

Azalea species;
Ghent Azaleas;
Mollis Azaleas;
Hybrids of Asian Azaleas;
Hybrid deciduous Azaleas;
Evergreen Hybrids.

Azalea species are, or should be, the genuine wild plants, in the same way as our Dog Rose and Sweet Briar are wild Roses. They are less common in gardens than the named garden varieties, though they are probably as beautiful.

Ghent Azaleas are hybrids and seem to owe their name to Montier (Pieter, I think), who was a baker in Ghent at the beginning of the nineteenth century. Not much seems to be known of him, so far as I have been able to find out, except that he was a dedicated gardener and a very clever plant breeder. Ghent Azaleas are tall, twiggy and usually very scented with a sweet honeysuckle fragrance. They flower about the end of May. Some Azaleas and Rhododendrons are expensive but the Ghent Azaleas are at least reasonable in cost.

Mollis Azaleas flower in early May and the flowers come before the leaves. They are short and bushy, about four feet or so in height, and are very beautiful when in full flower. Generally they come in yellow and orange shades.

Ghent and Mollis varieties are often doubles, which means they do not set seeds. This is claimed to be an advantage because the plants will not exhaust themselves by producing seeds. It is generally advised that members of the Rhododendron family that set seeds should have the seed heads nipped off after flowering. I have never been able to find time to do this and I have not found the shrubs lacking in vigour. The doubles flower in May and June and are usually fragrant.

The various hybrids are all beautiful shrubs, and there are some marvellous colours. In the mass they can be dazzling, almost barbaric. If it were not that in some gardens, where there may be traces of lime, they can be temperamental, by now somebody would have decided such abundance of brilliant colour is vulgar, but so far nobody has complained. Two famous strains of hybrids are Exbury Hybrids and Knap Hill Hybrids, named after the gardens where they were first raised. All I can say of them is that they are very beautiful, very rich in colour and if you use the pin-choosing method of picking them you can hardly make a mistake. A better method is to visit a nursery where they have a good collection.

Evergreen hybrids are of mixed parentage but the majority, possibly the best, came from Japan. The Kurume varieties are the best known. They are shrubs for light shade, but do observe that qualifying word 'light'. A few are on the tender side so a spot out of cold winds is advised for them, also they like the cool moist root runs that you find among trees and larger bushes.

There are no cultural secrets to be revealed. On the other hand you cannot just shove them in anywhere. Soil must be lime-free; that is essential. If there is lime present you can grow them in raised beds of peaty compost, though there is the risk of roots getting down to where there *is* lime – in time. On the other hand, if the lime is not a part of the soil of the district it is an ingredient that washes out from soils to which it has been added. Where a very little lime is present you can sometimes neutralise it by watering with Sequestrene or some similar substance. I have not tried it: some gardeners have used it with success; a few without.

Most Azaleas, as already mentioned, do well in light shade. The soil should be well-drained but never wet; they appreciate mulches of peat and compost from time to time. I use grass clippings myself, tipping one good boxful over each bush occasionally. *Over* the bush: messy, perhaps, but wind and the rain work it into the heart of the plant and it seems to do them good. Pruning you can keep to a minimum, removing unsightly shoots, weak spindly ones and dead ones. On the other hand, you can cut each bush back quite hard after flowering and it will renew its youth with young healthy branches. Although I do not nip out dead flower heads most growers agree that this is a good practice.

The Azalea grown as a pot plant is *Rhododendron simsii*, but is commonly called *Azalea indicum*. There are countless named varieties and they are all tender though they can spend the summer out of doors. Growing them for the florists' trade is a specialised branch of gardening and depends on correct soil, temperature, potting and so on. Amateurs, without the facilities and the necessary knowledge are often disappointed when the pot plant given them for Christmas does less well than expected, but persuading them to go on in a modest way is not an impossible task. Though indoor shrubs do not come within the scope of this book many readers may like to know some simple form of treatment. It may be summarised thus: a moderate growing temperature: careful watering so that the peat compost *never* dries out, though it must never be wet or cold; removal to a cool greenhouse to rest after flowering; plunging the pot in a cool shady bed in summer; bringing indoors to gentle warmth in autumn. Do not ever force in high temperatures but let the little bush flower naturally and slowly in its own good time.

So back to the great outdoors once more.

Most gardeners will make their own choice but I know there are others who like some guidance for a start. Obviously I cannot recommend more than a few favourites, so here are some I would plant myself:

Species (I have used *Azalea* as the specific name – it should be *Rhododendron* of course!):

Azalea atlanticum   American, 2-foot bush, May flowering, flushed with pink. Scented.

A. kaempferi   Strong growth, semi-evergreen, brilliant orange-red. June–July.

A. luteum (*A. pontica*)   Called the 'common' yellow in one list but my word what a beauty. Covered with blossom as scented as a honeysuckle and the autumn colour is even more rich than the blossom.

A. occidentalis   White flowers, yellow blotch, fragrant, June flowering.

A. rosea   Rose pink, strongly scented.

A. viscosum   White. Fragrant. July flowering.

Six only, but a good start to any collection.

Exbury Hybrids. A good way (and the cheapest) is to buy a collection of seedlings; you can hardly go wrong. Good named varieties are Berry Rose (Rose Pink), Cecile (Salmon-orange), Embley Crimson, Embley Orange, Hotspur (red), Townhill Yellow.

Knapp Hill Hybrids. There is not much to choose between these and the Exbury hybrids, but again six that could hardly disappoint anybody.

Fireglow (orange-vermilion), Harvest Moon (pale yellow), Persil (white; how did you guess!), Satan (dark red), Seville (orange), Westminster (pink).

Azaleas were introduced to this country from America about 1680 by Henry Compton, Bishop of Oxford, from seeds or plants sent to him by John Bannister, a missionary in Virginia and the species was *A. viscosum*, the Swamp Honeysuckle. But of course the story started thousands of years before that. There are species native to Europe. I have seen them on the Pyrenees, ten thousand feet up (out of flower, alas!), as thick as Winberries on a Radnorshire hillside. If you care to go back three thousand years you can read how Azaleas, probably *A. pontica* (*luteum*) nearly changed the course of history. The defeated army of Cyrus led by Xenophon fought in retreat from Babylon to the Black Sea. (About 40 BC.) Near Colchis (scene of the Golden Fleece legend) they robbed beehives of honey to help out the rations. No doubt after a fairly austere diet they had a right good feast. And then ensued 'vomiting, purging, delirium and coma'. By good luck they were not attacked while in this weakened state and apparently they all recovered. Pliny said the honey was made from the Oleander, but in his time the Oleander *was* an Azalea and later writers have identified the plant as *A. luteum*. It was not the first time Azalea honey had upset delicate stomachs: it was not the last. Used moderately it has been good in medicines. Cases of poisoning I am told still occur in the Caucasus. So that delicious scent that greets you on a hot day as you get near the old yellow Azaleas may not be as harmless as it seems. Even the Alpine species are said to cause headaches. No Rose without a thorn, but I have never heard bee-keepers worry about Azaleas. BERBERIS   We are well-launched among the shrubs now and no mistake about it. After Azaleas, the Berberis family. This genus contains somewhere near 500 species. Enough is enough, but 500 is too much. You can cut that down to about 150, give or take a few, that you could have in the garden. Still more than you want? Well one of my favourite nurseries lists about 50 and all species (which means not named garden varieties), so there is surely something for everybody.

Years ago a neighbour brought home a couple of bushes of a spiny shrub and gave me one. They had been given to him and he said the name was Jaundice Bush. I did not know it. Very few nurseries sell it now for a reason I will explain in a minute, but I took it the name indicated a herbal use – which it did. I identified it at last as *Berberis vulgaris*, once a common shrub, wild in some districts, but now practically exterminated. Another name was Pipperidge Bush – an old English title which Turner in the sixteenth century spelled 'Pypryge' – and others were Guild Tree, Rilts and Woodsour. It has been known and used from very ancient times and no doubt Woodsour was used because the berries and leaves and bark, I believe, are sour and astringent. I think it was Pliny who said it would 'stay the flux of the belly'. The Egyptians made of them a medicine for fever. The berries were for long used as a pickle 'to trimme or set out dishes of fish or flesh in broth', for making a jelly, in punch, and in other similar ways. Tusser mentions it in his *Five Hundreth Pointes of Good Husbandry* (1573) 'Conserves of Barbaries, quinces and such with sirops that easeth the sickly so much.' The leaves in a sauce were useful for 'soure belchings of choller' and the bark, as already indicated, was good as a remedy for jaundice. It was used in tanning leather, and in a hair-dye. Dr Lindley, whose library was left to the Royal Horticultural Society, thought the flowers showed an elementary nervous system because they are sensitive, the stamens closing in on the stigma at the least touch. Later botanists decided that this was a pollinating device, but even so Dr Lindley might have had the right idea.

This pretty and common shrub has yellow flowers and the prettiest coral-red elongated berries. I have read that they are too sour for birds: but my birds must like their fruit a little sharp for they eat them promptly. Once found everywhere, it is now hardly ever seen in the wild. The trouble is the Corn Blight, the Black Rust that attacked and ruined crops of wheat from time to time. It had been recognised from ancient times that there was some connection between the Blight on the Corn and the Barberry though nobody knew exactly what it was. Some said one thing, some another, but it was the mid-nineteenth century before the trouble was sorted out. The Black Rust has two stages of growth and one of these only is found on the Barberry. Where the climate is unfavourable to rusts the shrub is harmless. It grew close to cornfields in Saffron Walden without harming them, but to be fair to the farmers where rusts flourished it could be a menace. They seem to have made a very determined attack on it, and they appear to have been very successful. It is still catalogued, but in the purple form and not all nurseries have that.

I seem to have spent a mighty long time with a shrub I cannot whole-heartedly recommend for all gardens, but man cannot live by bread alone – I'm not referring to the wheat rust, though it does fit in – and it is one of our most interesting shrubs.

Only *B. vulgaris* is (or was) the culprit, though I am told all Barberries are frowned on if not forbidden in the U.S.A. You can plant any of a score of others with a clear conscience.

As you are hardly going to put in my nurseryman's whole collection, which will you choose? One of the best has now been exiled from the family and is called *Mahonia acquifolium*. I think my favourite is *B. darwinii*, discovered by Charles Darwin in Chile during the voyage of the *Beagle* and named after him. It is one of the loveliest of shrubs. It makes a dense little evergreen bush up to seven feet or so tall. The leaves are like miniature Holly leaves, the flowers are a rich deep yellow and the berries are purplish black. To see it at its best you should have single specimens but it will make an excellent hedge.

B. stenophylla a hybrid, with *B. darwinii* as one of its parents, is another very good one to grow. Here again is an excellent hedge or screen shrub, but to see it at its best you want single specimens. The habit is quite different from that of *B. darwinii* for it sends out long branches that arch gracefully. That means it has a wide spreading habit and it should be allowed ample room. The leaves are small, the spines quite formidable, the flowers which come in April–May are yellow and the berries dark-blue covered with a white bloom.

Other good evergreen kinds are *B. linearifolia* and *B. lologensis*, both of which are similar to *B. darwinii*. *B. verruculosa* is smaller and neater, up to four feet in height, and is sometimes used in the rock gardens.

Most of the deciduous species bloom in spring, and all the ones I know have flowers in some shade of yellow. The berries are often black but the colour is more varied than in the flowers. Some colour well in autumn and my first choice would always be *B. thunbergii atropurpurea*. While most of the Barberries colour well in autumn this one has deep purple foliage all the time it is in leaf. There are sub-species *erecta*, *superba* and so on and even to the poorest Latin scholar these titles tell their own tale.

Out of all the others I'm sure your own choice from nursery or catalogue will be as good as mine, and there are few not worth trying, but among the best are *B. aggregata* and *B. wilsonae*, while if you want one with a distinctive label for name-dropping, plant *B. brevipaniculata* which is one of the finest of the lot for autumn colour.

BUDDLEIA   I do not know why but at one time I had an idea that this shrub had some connection with Buddha, possibly because a lot of people called it Buddle Bush. It had not, of course; it was named, many years after his death, in honour of the Rev. Adam Buddle, a seventeenth–eighteenth century Rector of the Essex village of North Fambridge. He was a botanist whose work was most appreciated when he was not around to enjoy the honour.

Most people know this lovely shrub. The most popular species is *Buddleia variabilis* or *B. davidii* (after the French missionary, Père David). It was introduced from China about 1890 or a year or so earlier. It is a tall strong-growing bush that is rather untidy and formless in habit and the best way to treat it is as you do the hybrid tea Roses, cutting it down hard each year after flowering, or in spring, when it will send up strong young branches that will flower freely in the summer, over quite a long period if dead flowers are removed – as they should be since they become brown and unsightly. The shrub is noted as a favourite hunting ground of butterflies and bees and all manner of insects which come in great numbers to feast on (or gather) nectar from the long purple spikes of scented flowers. The colour is variable, shading from the palest lavendar to the deepest reddish-purple. At first the latter colour seems the most desirable, but if you have one or two of these then the contrast of a few pale shades is not a bad idea. There is one with white flowers. Buddleias will grow almost anywhere and in any soil. Good stiff London clay and the hotch-potch of city fumes seem to suit them to perfection: it is well known how seedlings sprang up in their hundreds on the bomb sites during and after the War. Another district where they seem happy in adversity is on the more arid, chalky thin-soiled spots in Hampshire – and there must be others. I would guess that they love warmth and a fair old baking in summer. I have never seen a seedling in my own garden.

There is plenty of choice of garden varieties. *B. davidii* Charming is pink, Fromow's Purple should be deep coloured enough for anyone and Royal Red also describes itself. White Cloud is white. (You could have guessed!) Nurseries will have a dozen or more besides these to choose from but don't worry overmuch about the name, choose the shade you want.

B. alternifolia bears flowers on year-old shoots, so what pruning has to be done must be carried out after flowering. Old wood should be thinned occasionally. *B. colvillei*, June flowering, also flowers on old wood. It is a native of the Himalayan foothills.

The other species commonly planted is *B. globosa*, a shrub from Chile, which has, as the name implies, ball-like inflorescences (groups) of scented yellow flowers. It is probably not as great a favourite as the Buddle Bush, and there have been some doubts as to its hardiness in the coldest districts. I do not think it is tender enough to worry about but the early flowers could suffer in a late spring frost. There is a hybrid between *B. davidii* and *B. globosa*. It is called *B. weyeriana* and the flowers are ball shaped and have a mixture of tints from both parents. Those who like it, like it: many gardeners are not impressed. There are also species with silvery leaves.

CALLUNA Because I was brought up in Pembrokeshire, by the sea at that, I always believed that Heather was the bell-flowered plant (*Erica*) that painted our cliff tops so rich a purple all late summer that you could believe some giant artist had dropped a paint pot on them. I was mighty indignant when, growing a little older and wandering farther afield, a cantankerous Scot informed me that ours was not Heather at all. The 'bonnie purple heather' of Scots poets (very few of them mentioned it actually!) unless you call Harry Lauder a poet, was the tiny-flowered species that we called Ling. And in Pembrokeshire we did not think a lot of Ling.

Anyhow, if name-switching is confusing anyone: the small-flowered Ling is *Calluna* (from the Greek word meaning to sweep) and is Scottish Heather; while the rather blousy Bell Heather (blousy according to my Scottish friend – and I've probably got Scots and Scottish all wrong too!) is *Erica*

I do not know that there are many true species of Ling. W. Keble Martin illustrates only one, *Calluna vulgaris*. But it makes up for that by the number of named varieties. There are all shades from the palest pink to a few reds such as C. W. Nix and white forms (lucky white Heather) are common. I have in my garden a white Bell Heather gathered by a Radnorshire lake, but that has never seeded itself; my Lings send up seedlings in abundance and many of them come a pure white. These are unnamed seedlings, but I also have bushes with white flowers, both single and double, which I bought from nurseries.

A curious fact, worth noting, is that the self-sown seedlings of Ling, in my Briar-patch, come in their hundreds on two banks in my garden, so thickly on one that we pull out the old woody plants to make room for the newcomers. But in no other part of the garden, though Rhododendrons grow and the soil is acid, do I ever find one solitary seedling.

Solomon named four things in life that he could never under-stand, the most famous, of course, being the way of a man with a maid (though with his thousand wives he should have): he might have added a fifth: the strange behaviour of those plants that never do as we would expect them to.

Ling is a plant for lime-free soil. I do not think there is any exception to that rule: there may be a few species which are more tolerant than others (as the winter-flowering Heathers, *Erica* are), but I have not seen them mentioned. They love peat, therefore ample moisture is indicated as desirable, but with me they make huge bushes on one bank that is always damp, yet do just as well on another where the Rhododendrons drain the soil almost to dust dryness. But peaty soil always.

As I have said, we have an abundance of seedlings so rather than prune I pull out bushes that look bare and unpromising. But if pruning is needed a light trimming of worn out branches can be carried out after flowering. On the Scottish moors where the young shoots are needed as food for sheep, and in places for grouse, they burn the old growth off in early spring. They always have done. Some of the rules about Heather burning date from 1400. They do it too in mid-Wales but I think have not done it as much of recent years. 'Setting fire to the hill' made quite a show once, when a dark night is illuminated suddenly by a glow, then by a sheet of flame that moves slowly over the hill a couple of miles away, lighting up a pillar of cloud that precedes it. No wonder these hill people accepted so readily the rich cadences of Biblical prose.

One of my earliest memories is being taken to tea at Tinkers Hill, a farm with acres of cliff and rough ground, that separated the cliff from the cultivated ground. Bell Heather and gorse were the only vegetation on it and for a special treat I was taken to 'burn the furze'. We each carried a bottle of paraffin and a dry stick. A gorse bush was set alight, after which we pushed our sticks into the paraffin bottle, lit it at a burning bush, then darted round setting fire to more bushes, the wind off the sea driving the flames and the smoke before us.

What joy it all was. How simple our pleasures.

Happy days!

Most Lings are low-growing and could best be used with other subjects, Lilies perhaps, that would not grow in lime soils (a few of them will). Or they could be used as ground cover under other and taller shrubs that dislike lime – Magnolia, Camellia, and a few more. Some Lings are erect and will grow into comparatively large bushes, two or even three feet high, but they get bare at the base and soon come to look old before their time. *C. hammondii* (white) grows taller than most, and *C. alportii* (crimson) is erect in form, and so is C. W. Nix, another crimson.

There is rather less choice of named varieties in this little shrub than in the Bell Heathers but a good half-dozen of the spreading or bushy ones are *C. elegantissims** (lilac); J. H. Hamilton, dwarf, pink; Mair's White, good for cutting; *C. pumila*, a white carpeter; *C. serlei rubra*, dark purple, and generally acknowledged to be the best of the family; H. E. Beale, which has long spikes of double rose pink flowers.

If you buy Heather honey from Scotland it is sure to be made from the nectar in Ling. Delicious stuff, but not above suspicion. Like the Azalea honey it can be rough on delicate digestions if you eat too much. This is no recent knowledge. William Turner (1538) said that 'Irica is a busshy tre lyke unto Tamariske, but much lesse, of whose floures bees make noughty honey.' And he was translating the Greek herbalist, Dioscorides. But the plant has been beyond reproach in other ways, useful to man and beast. It could be used as a thatch; the thatch could be secured by Heather ropes; it made a fine springy bed in the cottage and the floor was swept by a Heather besom. It was used in tanning leather and in dying wool yellow. It was fuel for the fire and an ingredient in Heather beer.

'He causeth the grass to grow for the cattle, and herb for the service of man.'

Now we can get it all at the supermarket. Much better!

Or not?

CAMELLIA   The best-known Camellia, which commemorates George Joseph Kamel, a seventeenth-century botanist missionary, is *Camellia sinesis*, the leaf of which is made into a well-known drink. It is a drink which Cobbett condemned bitterly.

'It has no useful strength in it; it contains nothing nutritious, besides being good for nothing it has badness in it . . . It is a weaker kind of laudanum which enlivens for the moment and deadens afterwards . . . the practice of drinking (it) must render the frame feeble and unfit to encounter hard labour or severe weather . . . it deducts from the means of replenishing the belly and covering the back. Hence succeeds a softness, an effeminacy,

---

* I have for simplicity's sake written these as species but they seem to be variations on *C. vulgaris* and should have *vulgaris* preceding the specific name as I give them. But to write *C. vulgaris serlei rubra* is being pedantic!

a seeking for the fireside, a lurking in the bed, and, in short, all the characteristics of idleness, for which, in this case, real want of strength furnishes an apology. The drinking (of it) fills the public house, makes the frequenting of it habitual, corrupts boys as soon as they are able to move from home, and does little less for the girls to whom the gossip of the table is no bad preparatory school for the brothel.'

Strong words! And what wicked brew encouraged innocent girls brothel-wards?

You'd never believe it – *Tea*!

Mr Cobbett preferred home-brewed beer. So did and do a lot of people. But the drink he disliked so much, made from a first-cousin of Camellia, has managed to hold its own.

The plants do well in sheltered places, say as wall plants, and the secret of success is never to plant in a spot facing east. The point is, the flower buds can stand a few degrees of frost, but if the early sun shines on them when they are frosted it thaws them out too quickly, cells burst and they then rot and die. If they are planted near a wall facing west they thaw out very slowly and as a rule are not damaged.

North of the Midlands, except near the sea, I expect it would be wise not to plant Camellias in the open but to use them as a plant for a cool greenhouse. That is what I do myself. It restricts you as to numbers but success is almost assured before you start. On my cold hillside I am sure I would have no luck outdoors with Camellias so I grow one only, Nagasaki, in half of a four-gallon cider barrel and it is a noble strong bush, crammed with double, rose-crimson blooms, streaked sometimes with white through most of March (when a bit of colour is much appreciated) and April. As soon as the flowers are over the tub goes outside and stays out until autumn. The bush is top-dressed with peat every year, and that is all. It is getting quite large now: I realise that there is an end to every honeymoon and that some day it will outgrow its tub and drop leaves or flower buds or indulge in some misbehaviour or other. But for the present I enlarge the tub by nailing a length of rubber hose round the rim each year and that gives just enough extra room for the peat top-dressing.

As to general garden culture, this is a shrub that dislikes lime, and flourishes in deep cool soils that contain plenty of peat and leafmould. It will tolerate some light shade, may even be the better for it, though dense shade of deciduous forest trees would be too much and it must be remembered that tree roots manage to get the best of the foods available in any soils.

Propagation is easy from cuttings taken in summer and they root most freely in the humidity of a propagation case, which can be no more than a deep box covered with glass. Buds can be used as cuttings – the short wooden spurs, of course, not flower buds – and where suitable branches grow, layers root easily and surely.

The most popular varieties are garden forms of *C. japonica*. There are singles and doubles and the colours shade from white through pinks to dark red. Any large nursery is likely to have a couple of dozen of these hybrids. A few very pleasant ones are *C. japonica alba simplex*, single, white; *A japonica elegans*, an old favourite, paeony-centred, light rose; Adolphe Audusson, another popular one, semi-double, red; Donckelari, semi-double, crimson, striped white; Noblissima, double white; *C. japonica magnoliaeflora*, shell pink, semi-double.

Of the others listed as species, not all of them are true species but hybrids. Some of them are very beautiful shrubs but are not always as showy as the japonica hybrids. *C. cuspidata* has small creamy flowers, *C. reticulata* has been praised as the most beautiful of the family but it is not as hardy as *C. japonica* and even in mild districts a wall position is the safest spot for it. *C. sasanqua* will flower in winter in favoured districts. It is one of the few scented kinds in the genus. *C. saluensis* is hardier than most, but the flowers are as susceptible to frost damage as any. *C. williamsii* is often listed as a true species but is a cross between *saluensis* and *japonica*. It is hardy and free-flowering and there are garden forms with pink flowers. The one called Donation is said to be the best.

The Camellia came to English gardens first in 1739 flowering in Lord Petres' garden at Thornton Hall in Essex. The introduction and reintroduction of various kinds is tied up with the Chinese tea trade and most of them were brought by the tea clippers, some through botanists and some by the clipper captains themselves, which goes to show that not all were keel-hauling bullies, who would not notice a pretty flower. The plant, though, had been grown in China, later Japan a thousand and more years earlier. As you would expect it has a fair share of legend. It owed its existence, according to the story, to an Indian mystic named Dharma. On one occasion when he should have been praying and meditating he fell asleep. To punish himself he cut off his bushy eyebrows and threw them on the ground. They took root and grew into the first tea plants, which possessed the property of making people alert and wakeful, and were a good stimulant for a tired mind.

CEANOTHUS This is one of the best blue-flowered shrubs we have; it has not much competition for there are not many good shrubs with blue flowers. Sad to say it is not as hardy as we would like it to be and it is difficult to grow in the colder parts of the country and even in mild places, better play safe and grow it on a warm wall. Perhaps the warning about tenderness has been stressed too often. The powder-blue hybrid grows with me, quite near a wall to be sure, but right on a corner where some bitter winds tear round at times but it has not appeared to suffer (so far!).

All the Ceanothus family come from North America. There are about fifty species. Some are deciduous, some evergreen. There are a few with white flowers but I cannot find that any of these are available. Anyhow, it is the blues we are interested in and they come in all shades from very light to dark, almost purple, while a couple of the garden hybrids are pinkish. Their home ground is roughly from California south to Mexico, where they thrive in the sunshine and light warm soils. No wonder they are inclined to be temperamental in our climate. But if you can get them acclimatised they are not particular as to soil, indeed have been used in America to halt soil erosion in hot and arid places.

The first Ceanothus to be grown in this country was the white flowered *C. americanus* which was grown by Bishop Compton at Fulham about 1713. So far as I know it is not grown now though it has been used in hybridising. One of its American common names was New Jersey Tea and a tea could be made from the leaves. The Red Indians drank it and called it pong-pong tea, which was derived from the Indian name, not the smell.

The most popular species is *C. dentatus* which is always safest in the shelter of a wall. It is evergreen with flowers of a satisfying deep blue. Some gardeners call it Californian Lilac on account of the scent, but the similarity ends there. It was introduced a little over a hundred years ago. As it flowers on old wood a little light trimming is the best pruning treatment – when it needs trimming.

C. Gloire de Versailles is deciduous, powder blue, and lilac-scented. It can be cut hard back to old wood and the young shoots that grow will flower in their first season. It does not matter when it is pruned but perhaps spring is better than autumn except where winters are exceptionally mild. In such districts it can go years with very little pruning and will then bear a heavy crop of bloom.

A few other species are available and a lot of hybrids. *C. burkwoodii* is a good summer-flowering form. Cascade is a hybrid and excellent in spring. Autumnal Blue, as the name indicates, flowers mainly in autumn. *C. lobbianus* is the same as *dentatus*, or practically so, and there does not seem much point in listing both, though many nurseries do.

C. thyrsiflorus is the hardiest of the race. This was the original Californian Lilac, though the name is used for the whole family now; it was discovered in 1815 by the Collector J. F. Eschscholz, after whom the Californian Poppy was named. It has bright blue flowers and grows rather tall, up to thirty feet where conditions suit it. Of course it can be cut back where height is not wanted, but for those who want an evergreen shrub with blue flowers to cover a high wall this is ideal.

Clematis montana growing over an old tree at Wyevale Nurseries

Rosa cantabrigensis, one of the most attractive of the Rose species, has single yellow flowers

Kalmias give a good account of themselves in lime-free soil

CERATOSTIGMA I cannot claim that this is either popular or common, though it would be both if more gardeners knew about it. It has the disadvantage that, as a shrub, it is tender, but, like a Fuchsia, if it is killed to the ground by frost it will usually shoot up renewed and full of vigour each spring. Originally it was called *Ceratostigana plumbaginoides*, then after being known as *Plumbago larpentae* in honour of Lady Larpent who grew the one plant in England sent from China by Robert Fortune about 1847. It became, hard as it is to believe, *Valoradia plumbaginoides*! Later it was shifted back to the original name, but the best plan is to call it Plumbago (Leadwort) and ask for Plumbago, Miss Willmot. If you enjoy the sonorous syllables you can say *Ceratostigma willmotianum*. Miss Willmot was a famous Victorian gardener and flower artist.

It makes a shrub about three feet tall; this variety is moderately hardy, so if you can spare it a bit of wall near the front door it should not be any trouble, though a few old fern fronds over it in the worst weather are a good insurance. The flowers are a deep intense blue. It likes good soil but there are no particular difficulties about cultivation. There is a species which is equally lovely. This is *C. griffithii* but this *is* tender and suitable only for the mildest districts.

CHAENOMELES This can be claimed as the one plant with which the gardner has beaten the botanist. It was originally, in 1784, known as *Pyrus japonica* when found in Japan. Since it was obviously more of a Quince than a Pear it then became *Cydonia japonica*. This name caught on: gardeners called it either Cydonia or Japonica, the second name became the more familiar; now the botanists could tear out their hair in handfuls but no sensible gardener would ever think of calling it anything else. It's easier to spell, too!

It has been cultivated widely in our gardens since the early nineteenth century. It is so well known that it is almost an insult to describe it. The flowers are like apple blossom but much more showy and to my mind the best ones, coming as they do almost before we have swept winter off the doorstep, are the deep reds.

C

But there are pink and orange shades and a lovely white, which seems to have no common name but has the aristocratic title of *Chaenomeles lagenaria nivalis*. But, as our roadman used to say of his daughter when told she much resembled her mother: we thinks none the worse of her for that.

In warm gardens the flowers come out well in advance of the leaves, so all is well. In mine, where spring can be coolish, the leaves sometimes come first. Then when you wonder what has happened to the flowers you move a few branches and lo and behold, the whole bush, under the leaves, is aflame with blossom. For gardeners who have wondered what to do in such circumstances I will mention that when colour can be seen in the buds I go over the bushes with shears and cut off all the long thin shoots that presently will be in full leaf. This seems drastic and cruel, but it passes the acid test: it works. The bushes flower beautifully and afterwards send up another thicket of twigs to bloom the next year.

Any of the Japonicas you can buy at the nursery are good and usually reliable. Among the best, and best-known, are Rowallane Seedling and Knap Hill Scarlet. A white has been mentioned. *C. lagenaria cardinalis* is pink. *C. japonica* should be orange but it is wise to check with the nurseryman, because sometimes that is listed as *Cydonia maulei*.

The bushes bear quince-like fruits, generally orange, very tempting to look at but hard as stones. If they are left on the bushes they are decorative in winter, while if they are picked they can be used for making Quince jelly.

CISTUS This is the Rock Rose. Its relation Helianthemum is also often called Rock Rose (sometimes Sun Rose) so some confusion has crept in. The difference is that Helianthemum is a tiny shrublet, inches high, generally grown in rock gardens, while the Cistus is about 3–4 feet high, and often as much through. The flowers are white, or pinkish, or white marked with pink, reddish or yellow blotches, and do resemble wild roses in shape and in size. They do not last more than a day or two at most, but there is a good succession of them. The Cistus is a very decorative and pretty shrub when and where it grows well.

Unfortunately, though reputedly easy, it does *not* always grow well. It is certainly on the tender side in cold or exposed gardens. I have lost plants after a hard winter. I do not know if they start up again from the root-stock in some gardens. They did not in mine. They are said to grow well in very dry conditions. I think this is the truth, but often the hot dry soils are barren ones, and those they do not like. I know because I tried it! So plant them in fertile well-drained soil in the hottest, sunniest spot you can find in a warm garden where the soil does not freeze iron-hard for a foot down. Do all that and you can join the ranks of those who swear the Cistus is as easy as it is lovely. In less genial climates choose the site with the greatest care and protect in vicious frosts. Otherwise, to adapt Queen Elizabeth's advice to Walter Raleigh:

> If thy heart fail thee
> Plant not at all.

But if you have seen them in all their glory on a Mediterranean hillside I think you will take a risk. Luckily they are very easy to raise from cuttings, so replacements can be plentiful and cheap. They hybridise very freely, so freely that there used to be a joke about their sex life and easy virtue. I suppose real experts might know which are true species and which are hybrids: on the other hand they might not. They were known to all the ancient writers on gardening, and to the Egyptians even earlier. Turner reported their growing at Syon House in 1548; they could well have been here centuries before; there is no clear record. Some species are scented and in a warm climate, where they grow freely, their fragrance can be smelt from a great distance. Napoleon, speaking of this scent, said he would know Corsica with his eyes shut. The most strongly scented are *C. ladaniferus* and *C. salicifolius*, neither of which I can find in any list. This is strange because they have been the source of a sticky scented gum, the manufacture of which is said to date back traceably to the First Dynasty in Egypt before 3,000 BC. It was called ladanum (not to be confused with the Poppy's laudanum) and was used in both perfumery and medicine. The perfume Chypre takes its name from the fact that Cyprus (chypre in French) was a noted source of it. There were various ways of collecting it, the most interesting being by combing it from the beards of goats that fed on the leaves. 'Whenas the gotes and gotes bucks eat the leaves of cistus they gather manifestly the fatness with their beards . . . the which the inhabiters of the countre combe of and streyne it, and make it in lumpes together and so lay it by.'

So wrote Turner. And suddenly I remember the only goat I knew well. It also had its smell, but it was not of chypre . . . but that is another story.

I believe plants of *C. ladaniferus* should be obtainable for it is commonly called Gum Cistus and it is sometimes recommended in books. As to the hybrids any large nursery will have from a dozen to a score in stock. *C. corbarious* is claimed to be fairly hardy. The buds are tinted red, the open flowers white. *C. cyprius* I do not know. It sounds as if it might be from Cyprus and so could be aromatic. It is fairly tall where it thrives, up to 7 feet perhaps, is hardier than most, and the flowers are white. For a variation in colour *C. pulverulentus* is dwarf (2 feet) and pink and *C. purpureus* is a shade of purple. Yellows are found in a related family (or maybe hybrids) known as Halimium. There are half a dozen kinds or species, *H. halimifolium* and *H. ocymoides* being a good couple to start with. *C. stolonifers flaviramea* has yellow bark, but is not as showy as *C. alba*.

CLEMATIS This climbing shrub is such a large family, and so important a family to the garden, that it needs a volume all to itself to do it justice. It probably has a few. I have one myself* that was published in 1962, exactly a hundred years since lovely, familiar, purple *Clematis jackmanii* was first introduced. To many gardeners *C. jackmanii is* clematis. They know no other and grow no other. Nobody could fail to know it, for it grows on hundreds of cottage walls and porches all over the country – over castle

* *Success with Clematis*, by J. Fisk (Nelson).

walls as well if it comes to that, but you can't always see those –
and all summer the great wide-open purple flowers are as familiar
as hedgerow primroses were earlier in the year. It is really a
hybrid but is generally listed as if it were a species.

The only native species is *C. vitalba*. Most Clematis have only
the Latin or botanical name (you'd think *jackmanii* would have
earned a popular nickname by now) but *C. vitalba* has two
popular names, and a score of local ones. Almost everyone must
have called it Traveller's Joy and nearly as well known is Old
Man's Beard. The more localised contain such labels as Grand-
father's Whiskers and Hedge Feathers, and since country lads
used to experiment in smoking it it got such titles as Boys' Bacca
and Shepherd's Delight. Gerard claimed it was he who gave it
the name Traveller's Joy. He said it was 'no use in physicke as
yet found out.' Probably he was correct for the Clematis belongs
to the Buttercup family, the Ranunculaceae, and they are a
poisonous tribe and should all be treated with suspicion. I have
read, but I cannot remember when or where, that the filaments
from Traveller's Joy (they are seed heads not flowers) can be a
very unpleasant lung irritant. I have a vague idea that somebody
had been using them as a stuffing for cushions or pillows.

True species reached this country at the end of the sixteenth
century. Mr Fisk says that the first was *C. viticella* which has
purple flowers. You can still buy a plant of that at any large
nursery, and there is a white, or whitish form, but it is doubtful
if there is a great demand. Others followed, mainly from America
and China. In the early nineteenth century Robert Fortune
brought *C. languinosa* from China. This was one of the parents of
jackmanii. *C. patens* came from Japan, and about this time hybridising began. I am no Clematis expert – in fact they do not like
my heavy Rhododendron–Heather soil – but I imagine that the
modern Clematis starts with *C. jackmanii*. Large-flowered hybrids
came along fast, many with flowers of poor colour – poor
purples are poor indeed. Some have died out but a lot are
available now in a great variety of rich shades and there are
excellent white varieties. In the easy-to-manage *iackmanii* section

are Comtesse de Bouchard, pink; Gipsy Queen, purple; Mme Edouard André, red; Mrs Cholmondeley, light blue; the President, purple; and of course no collection should omit *jackmanii*, the grand-daddy of them all. Not all nurseries may have that particular half-dozen but you can be sure they will have some equally as good.

Anyone interested in growing this climbing shrub will find plenty of material from which to make a collection. There are uncommon species that are difficult to obtain and new ones – perhaps only to be seen at Royal Horticultural Society Shows – come along fairly steadily. Jackmans, who still specialise in the genus have some four pages of species and hybrids listed in their catalogue, also, incidentally, a couple of pages of good advice on cultivation.

The ordinary gardener will want a few of the best and most showy ones and for him the choice narrows down to a few groups. Jackmans give 10 groups but even that is more than you will find, or want, in most gardens.

C. montana is the relatively small-flowered species with blossoms (they are actually sepals, not petals) a couple of inches across in early summer. They are white or, rather less popular, a light purple. The plant needs a minimum of pruning, in fact, well-grown specimens will cover the side of a house or grow all over a dead or unwanted tree, so you cannot prune much even if you wanted to.

The *jackmanii* group is the most popular, and has the largest, most showy flowers. If you like to be pedantic you can include the *viticella* group with these because they need similar pruning. They should be cut back hard each year in early spring and will flower on the new wood. This is 'correct' pruning but there is a point to note here. Many country gardeners have been growing *C. jackmanii* for years and the plants have never even seen a pruning knife. You can see these creeping up a hundred arches over cottage doors and they flourish exceedingly.

So, to interrupt the flow of what I hope is the good advice I have to offer, if you do not or cannot prune your plants at all there is no occasion to worry. They are almost certain to do as well without attention as with.

Of course if you don't prune the *jackmanii* section they will flower at the ends of rather bare stems but for growing on arches that may be all to the good.

Some of the family flower on wood that grew the previous year. Obviously the method here will be to cut back a little after flowering, so that those shoots can have a good chance to establish themselves. The florida group and the patens group are treated so. They are similar in appearance to *jackmanii*, a little smaller, I think, and just as brilliant. A lot of gardeners grow, and recognise, Nellie Moser: well, she is in the *patens* section. A good example of the *florida* lot is the lovely white Duchess of Edinburgh.

But the various groups have been intermingled and cross-bred over the years and I do not think, unless we are aspiring to be specialists, the differences matter to us very much so long as we do not cut any of the florida or patens group to ground level every year. There is an important *languinosa* section (*C. languinosa* and its hybrids) that very obligingly will flower on new or old wood.

Really what it boils down to is: when uncertain, leave alone.

A great many of the large-flowered types are grafted on to stocks of *C. viticella*. Traveller's Joy also is used as a stock, and I believe is the more usual nowadays. There must be a good reason for this but nobody has ever told me, or been able to tell me, what it is. The great disadvantage is that very occasionally the graft fails, early in life or late, and the grafted part dies. William Robinson, as clever a gardener as he was crusty, said nurserymen's plants died off like flies. Since almost any Clematis will grow easily from cuttings and even more easily from layers, there seems no reason at all why we should not have the plants on their own roots. If you propagate in either way remember, unlike most shrubs, Clematis form roots most freely from the bare stem *between* the leaf nodes, *not* just under a bud.

They do not transplant easily so should whenever possible, whether grafts, cuttings or layers, be propagated in pots from which they can be moved with the minimum of root disturbance.

As for growing, there are a couple of points worth remembering. Clematis like a warm, well-drained soil; they need plenty of nourishment so an annual mulch of old manure or similar material in early spring is good for them. Most of the family appear to thrive when there is plenty of lime in the soil. If you can beg, borrow or steal – or even buy if absolutely necessary – a barrow-load of old mortar rubble from a builder's yard, that will be just the thing. Some experts say lime is not *essential*.

Clematis like to have their heads in the sun, their feet in the shade, so they can be planted near shady walls, or have their roots under low shrubs such as Lavender or Santolina, or even have a bit of crazy-paving around them.

Guard against slugs if the plants have been hard pruned. Why none of the poisonous plants disagree with slugs I do not know – but apparently they do not.

And one lovely little last tip. Jackmans say a mulch of old tea-leaves is strongly recommended. They should know.

CORNUS This is the Dogwood family and the members of it vary from small shrubs to forest trees. The shrubs can hardly be considered the most beautiful or the most valued in the shrub garden, but they are easy and grow anywhere and can be a great help where the odd unpromising corner has to be filled. *Cornus mas* is the Cornelian Cherry, easy, with small flowers towards the end of winter. It grows to tree size. The berry crop seems to be an uncertain dividend, though I cannot speak with authority on that point. Some experts say they do fruit easily; some say they don't. I suppose we could say the same of Apples or Plums. They must be satisfactory in some areas for they were planted as fruiting trees some 400 years ago. Thomas Tusser gave advice on the time to plant, calling them 'cornet pluma'. Parkinson said 'by reason of the pleasantnesse in them when they are ripe they are much desired.' John Evelyn knew how to pickle the fruit so that they would pass for Olives and earlier Turner had said something similar; later again Bryant recommended them for 'tarts and other devices'.

I don't think anybody plants *C. mas* for its fruit any more, but what has been done can be done again and a change, as our roadman said when his wife left him, is even better than a rest.

Some Dogwoods have variegated foliage. About the best of these is *C. alba spaethii*, easy and very decorative if you like variegated leaves.

I consider the best of the family is the one with red stems, which also, strangely is *C. alba*, 'alba' being white. The one to use is *C. alba sibirica*. It is a spreader and is not really suitable for very small gardens. If you have a large garden and there is a rough corner where little else will thrive, plant this red-stemmed Dogwood. Cut it down to the ground each spring so that you get a good crop of healthy young shoots. In summer you can forget it, but when autumn comes and the leaves fall there will be a mass of stems of the richest shining crimson. And it will gladden your heart all winter long with its warm colour. If you can possibly have it in view from a window you can cheer yourself up on the coldest winter day by looking at it, while against snow or in thin winter sunshine it positively glows.

But you *must* cut it down each spring.

'It'll spread, you know!' said the Candid Critic.

So it will; but you can pull out what you don't want and give some to your friends. After all, the nurseries will charge you up to ten bob for it!

CORONILLA Here, if you have a warm garden is a little gem, easy to grow, easy to obtain, and with a flowering season that lasts from early summer until late autumn.

My father, whose garden was near the sea, had against a wall a smallish shrub with rather twisted, gaunt branches which all summer long were loaded with rich yellow pea-shaped flowers. They were about the size of Birds-foot-trefoil, if you know that pretty wild flower, and the leaves were light green. He told me that it was *Coronilla glauca* and that he had grown it from a cutting somebody gave him. It was easy from cuttings, and he often rooted a shoot or two to give away. I found three of these rooted cuttings, in pots on, of all places, the bathroom window-

ledge and when I asked if I could have one he said I could take
the lot. So I did – and a warning that it was extremely unlikely
that they would stand outside conditions in *my* garden.

Well I grew these little trees in their pots (fair-sized ones) for
year after year in the greenhouse and always they thrived and
always they flowered for half a year or more. But you know how
it is – in the garden as in life – you don't value truly the friends
who are kindest to you, and one year something simply *had* to
go outside to make way for thrusting newcomers, so I searched
out the sunniest, warmest corner I had and planted out my little
Coronillas, hoping for the best.

But *hoping* for the best really is not enough. We must deserve
it (I think I've quoted that already!).

They died!

If you have a really warm garden somewhere south of the
Thames (no, not on the windswept Downs), and a nice warm
wall try *Coronilla glauca* and you will not be disappointed. And
if you live north of the river and want a good shrub for a tub
that you can take into a cold greenhouse for the winter, then
C. glauca will please you also.

Otherwise anyone may try *C. emerus* (though I do not know
who stocks it), which is hardier, but rather less dainty. It is
probably most reliable in seaside districts. It will, however,
thrive in any soil, even on the hungriest of chalks.

COTONEASTER This is a most important family of shrubs, not
for their flowers – which at the best are inconspicuous, at their
worst, downright dingy – but for the brightness and brilliance of
their berries. Some species are deciduous, some evergreen; others,
clinging to their leaves through most of the winter, are not able
to make up their minds what they are. There are a few European
species but it does not seem certain that any are British. One or
two may be but the whole tribe interbreed pretty freely and I
have an idea that many listed as species (originals you might say)
are the fruit of cross-pollination. I know in my garden I have only
a few but I find seedlings coming up in out-of-the-way places
like crevices in walls. These are probably from seeds the birds

drop. Most of the popular kinds are from that Paradise of the nineteenth century plant hunters, north-eastern India to south-western China, and most have come during the last hundred years or so. *Cotoneaster frigida*, one of the oldest, came through the good offices of the East India Company as early as 1824 but the best-known and most common, *C. horizontalis* (which anyone should recognise by its name), came as late as 1874, and many, less familiar, have been introduced much later.

There are some 60 or so species and varieties we may grow in our gardens and of these a remarkably high number are actually listed in catalogues. I have a list with over 40 different ones. The mystery is who buys 'em because you do not seem to see more than two or three different kinds, and those the most familiar, in any garden. But if you want them you can have them, and a gardener with lots of room to spare might do worse than set aside a piece of ground for a thicket of these fine berry-bearing plants. It might keep the birds busy, too, and away from the fruit buds and, which they love most of all, the polyanthus flowers.

Some of the Cotoneasters are good open-ground plants and are useful for specimens. Since they are generally grown for their berries they should be planted where they are in full view from the window of a much lived-in room, and then no matter how much blood be nipped and ways be foul you can enjoy them in comfort.

But most gardeners know Cotoneasters best as wall shrubs. They are not true climbers, many species are prostrate ground-hugging shrubs, but planted near a wall they will obligingly flatten themselves and grow upwards. Put it this way: planned by nature for the horizontal, they like the vertical equally well. *C. horizontalis* is the best-known, but *C. frigida* is equally good or even better. I heard that it has the common name of Architect's Friend because it will cover an unsightly wall completely and so well. Alas, I don't think the common name has spread as easily as do its branches for Cotoneasters are among those well-known shrubs which, strangely, never seem to gain the familiarity of nicknames. William Robinson suggested Rock Spray for some of the so-called climbers, but I've never heard the name used.

Out of the mixture that a large nursery could offer you, you would not go far wrong if you started on the following half-dozen.

C. adpressa is a small species, often used in a rock garden. It has bright red berries and the leaves turn scarlet in autumn.

C. franchetti has grey leaves and scarlet berries. This might be used as a specimen bush. Any of those with upright habit can, of course, be used in this way but some are better than others.

C. frigida. Another useful as a bush and very reliable with its crimson fruit. A good shrub for cold districts; it got its name because of the coldness of the region of northern Nepal, where it was found.

C. horizontalis. To use that lazy description so often used by the herbalist Nicholas Culpeper (though not of this red-berried shrub) 'too well-known to merit description.' It is best grown flat against a wall.

C. microphyllus is evergreen, quite small but with good-sized berries and a good wall plant.

C. simonsii is a fairly common variety. I had a wall specimen once and it had an enormous spread and went up and up. I had to move it at last because it wanted the whole wall for itself. It seeds itself a lot – or the birds sow it – and as a rule there are plenty of replacements if you look for them. In the open I have found it a little over-stiff in form, too-straight of branches, like a sergeant major on parade, but it is a valuable and easy shrub and reliable in berry and brilliant leaf-colour.

CRATAEGUS I am now on dangerous ground. This is the Haw-thorn or May; it is a tree rather than a shrub and a mighty big tree too where it is suited. Not all gardens would have room for even one fully grown specimen. But it is such a lovely thing, both in flower and in berry, and it responds easily to hard pruning, so room could be found for at least one specimen. It is a native too – 'Oak, Ash and Thorn' – easy to grow, very hardy, usually strongly scented; a tree we would value more highly if it were rare, foreign and difficult. It belongs to the Rose family, is closely related to the Apple, and the fruits or haws you will find, if you examine them closely, are very much the same in appearance, though not at all in flavour. They are edible, though they do not taste of anything in particular, and when we were children we used to chew them for want of anything better. The chewing-gum age had not arrived, nor would we have had the money for that, so I suppose there is a chewing instinct inborn in us.

There are a dozen Thorns I could offer. Thorns with thorns, Thorns with vicious extra-large thorns, and Thorns without thorns; Thorns with large haws, Thorns with small ones; Thorns with scarlet haws, Thorns with yellow haws. There are some with upright habit, and also weeping varieties; some have leaves deeply lobed, some hardly at all.

I think we will limit the choice to two, one a native wild species, the other a garden variety which has been developed from it – though some claim it is a different species.

Crataegus monogyna is the British May, as familiar as oak. It grows easily anywhere, can be pruned back to fit in to any size, flowers in white reliably, is deliciously scented and most years bears a heavy crop of scarlet berries. Birds eat the berries but maybe, like small boys, eat them when there is nothing else available. Countrymen always claim that a heavy crop of Haw-thorn berries foretells a hard winter and is Nature's way of providing food for the birds. It is a pleasant superstition, so many are not, but Nature could help the birds (and us) equally well by sending a mild winter; so as a means of weather forecasting it is not reliable.

After a mild winter the berries stay on the trees until late spring and when they fall on good ground, carried on a spring gale or by birds or a small boy, will germinate and grow easily. Hawthorn is one of our best hedging shrubs and though if you want a hedge you can buy young plants cheaply, you can equally well raise your own from seed, or, if you have the patience, grow the hedge *in situ* from seed.

There is a species *C. monogyna stricta*, sometimes listed as *C. fastigiata*, that is said to be smaller and more compact.

If you examine the flowers closely you will find, unlike the washing advertisements, that some are less 'whiter than white'. They have a hint of pink. Few are distinctly pink. Breeding and selecting have turned this characteristic to good effect and given us the crimson-flowered form. Again there is uncertainty as to whether it is a true species or a sub-species. The best one is usually listed *C. oxyacantha* and the one to go for is *C. oxyacantha coccincea plena*. This is the Crimson Thorn, double and a very beautiful little tree in flower. But you cannot have everything and the Crimson Thorn has lost most or all of its scent and being double does not bear berries. In the same way as the whites vary in shade, so do the crimsons, so if possible choose the tree when in flower at a nursery, or you may get only a deep pink. In fact *C. oxyacantha rosea flore plenaa* is pink, and if you prefer pink that is the one to choose.

The Hawthorn has a wonderful literature gathered round it and is as well embedded in folklore and herbalism as any native tree. John Evelyn in his *Sylva* recommends it mainly for fencing and spent many pages in describing how Thorn hedges could and should be grown. He had little to say of it as a forest tree but C. A. Johns in *The Forest Trees of England* (around 1856) has a couple of engravings of enormous specimens, the Newham Thorn, and the Hethel Thorn. The latter it was claimed was mentioned in a deed dated some time in the thirteenth century. Johns tried to find the deed but was unsuccessful. No doubt this was a local tradition but no doubt also the tree was a very ancient one.

John collected a number of superstitions that had grown up round the Thorn. The old country belief that it was unlucky to bring the flowers into a house before the month of May is fairly well known. Not so common is the belief that the tree groans and sighs on the evening of Good Friday. This no doubt is connected with the Crown of Thorns. There was a tree growing over a holy well in County Wicklow on which the people hung shreds of clothing on the day of St Kevin. Now that, as far as I know, has never been explained, but Darwin in his *Voyage of the Beagle* observed an almost identical custom somewhere near the Rio Negro, and similar practices have been observed in other parts of the world.

Evelyn said the wood was 'excellent both for boxes and combs and is curiously and naturally wrought'. He mentioned also that the timber had been used for ribs for small boats. Evelyn sometimes seems a little humourless: 'It was accounted among fortunate trees, and therefore used in *Faces Nuptiarum*, since the jolly shepherds carried the White Thorn at the Rapine of the Sabines.'

One could understand the shepherds being jolly. They would be the lads Romulus had brought to collect wives but it wasn't so jolly or fortunate for those buxom Sabine women in the famous Rubens picture.

Or could it have been!

The nicest Thorn tree story is about the Glastonbury Thorn. Briefly, it relates how, after the Crucifixion, Joseph of Aremathea and other disciples left Palestine carrying with them the Holy Grail, the Cup that had been used at the Last Supper. They wandered far and wide and at last came on a Christmas Day to Glastonbury. Joseph knew when they got there that that was the end of the journey and as a sign he thrust his Thorn staff deep into the soil. At once it took root, and there, before their eyes, it sent out branches and the branches flowered.

There are descendants of that tree in various parts of England. I know of one in Herefordshire and there are still old people who believe it does flower on Christmas Day, old style.

CYTISUS 'There was an old man and he lived in a wood
And his trade it was gathering of broom, green broom.'

So goes the ballad. And why was he gathering it? Undoubtedly to make brooms or besoms, by selling which, if you don't know the song, was how his lazy son John found a rich and beautiful young wife.

He could, as a sideline, have gathered some for making medicines. Gerard gave it a qualified approval as a herb. He said the flower buds could be used in salads, but as medicine pointed out that it could 'by reason of his sharpe quality many times hurt and fret the entrails.'

In Pembrokeshire, years ago, Broom definitely was regarded as poisonous. I think I have already mentioned that the seeds of many legumes are suspect; even the edible ones are indigestible if taken too freely. There was a queer superstition of the ancient Greeks that Broad Beans contained the souls of people who had died and so they must not be eaten. The legend about the end of Pythagoras, the mathematician, was that he was caught by his enemies because he would not cross a Bean field, for fear of damaging plants which contained living souls. All these old legends have a common source somewhere.

Earlier Turner cautiously said it should not be taken inwardly 'except the patient were very stronge'.

Well, quoting our roadman again, 'to make a long story longer', the time came when I had a very large rough piece of ground around my garden. It had two (and only two) good features. A tiny stream flowed through it and there was a rough shale bank on which Broom bushes grew by the score. Between spring and summer they flowered and there never was such a torrent of gold as poured down that little hillside.

One day old Roberts the Gwystre, who was much wiser than most people gave him credit for, came and asked could he gather Broom tips from my bushes. I said, yes of course, and asked him what he wanted them for. He said it was for making medicine – it was either for his heart or his kidneys – maybe both! – which, believing it to be a poisonous plant, surprised me. Anyhow, the old chap lived for many years after that, so either he had a very strong constitution or the Broom was not as poisonous as I had believed. Culpeper had a dozen uses for it: 'Flegm, Joynts, dropsie, Sids (pains in the side?), Spleen, Bladder, Kidnies, Stone, Disury (?), black Jaundice, Agues, Toothach, Wind, Stitches, Lice.'

He does mention 'It provoketh strong Vomits'; perhaps, as with Laburnum, it is the seeds that are the trouble.

Gerard says 'That worthy prince of famous memory Henry 8,

King of England, was wont to drinke the distilled water of Broome floures, against surfeits and diseases therof arising.'

That could mean it was taken after over-eating: it could mean other things, but in the 1590s when Gerard was writing, you were cautious what you said about 'that worthy Prince . . . Henry 8.'

Brooms are excellent shrubs for hot dry soils. If you can establish them (preferably from seed), they will grow, even flourish, in places where the soil is so arid that even Stonecrops will not look too happy. On fertile soil they are still good shrubs but are not always long-lived, so it pays to keep a stock of seedlings in reserve. They have a reputation for not transplanting well, so the seeds are generally sown singly in small pots. But this also may be a superstition. In my garden they seed themselves freely – generally in gravel paths, where I do *not* want them. Visitors ask if they can have these seedlings and I say, certainly, but warn that it is unlikely that the little plants will live. But they always do, so the accepted view that they do not transplant may be another of those handed-down fallacies that gardeners are prone to repeat without testing.

There are many Brooms in the catalogues and in the nurseries. None, I am sure, is more beautiful than our own native *Cytisus scoparius*. Next I would put *C. alba*, the White Broom (one catalogue calls it 'Portuguese', another 'Spanish'. A whole new range of colours has been developed and at first glance they seem exciting but after looking at them hard and carefully I still think common Broom leads. There are other white ones beside *C. alba;* there is Andrés Broom with red wings, and many named hybrids with the same variations of red wings and yellow or white wings. There are dwarf species, *C. procumbens*, for example, or *C. kewensis* in white, or *C. versicolor*, buff and lilac. New hybrids appear every year, some of which are worth a place in any garden, but, as with so many plants, not all that is new is better. More of a curiosity than a beauty is *Laburnocytisus adamii* which is a graft of *C. purpureus* on Laburnum. It produces (sometimes) some yellow flowers and some purple.

I was told that Cytisus was being renamed *Sarothamnus*. I cannot believe it! Even botanists could not be so unkind. I cannot find *Sarothamnus* in any list and I cannot see much chance of it being used, except in botanical treatises, for many years to come. DABOECIA It is a pity this could not have been left among the Ericas, where Linnaeus first placed it because it is so obviously a Heather. If I seem to have an obsession about these names – and the name of this little 2-foot shrub has been altered enough – it is because you can so easily get the plant you do not want. Some call Daboecia, Irish Heather but that in most books is *Erica vagans*. There are a number of common names in its native Ireland, the best known being St Daboec's Heather. Fair enough, but how do non-Irishmen pronounce Daboec? Show the name to half a dozen gardeners and they all come out with something different, all rather hesitantly.

Only one species of this lovely Heather is commonly grown. It is *D. cantabrica* and it is available in white and purple, or with rather changeable flowers of both colours. The white variety is larger than our own Heathers and the flower stems are quite striking. Alas Daboecia is rather tender though in all but the coldest gardens it is worth a try if you give it a warm sheltered position.

D. azorica is smaller, and it is even more tender.

DAPHNE There is a score of these shrubs that can be grown in the garden but some are uncommon and some are difficult and I think they are all a bit temperamental. Some will grow well and flourish in certain gardens while a hundred yards away they sulk, refuse to flower, even die without apparent reason. In my own plot *Daphne laureola*, which is supposed to resemble a Laurel (it would be a very small one), grows freely. It is not at all spectacular as it has green or greenish flowers, but it is sweetly scented in the evenings. It is not a shrub I would specially recommend but it grows in an uncultivated corner, almost a wild garden, and seeds itself so I just leave it alone. There is little doubt that it is a native; it was described by Turner in 1548, when it was grown largely for medicinal purposes, though

Miller said the poor people collected it in the woods to sell in towns.

The best known is *D. mezereum*, another native. It is a small shrub with either purple or white scented flowers borne tightly down the stems very early in spring or even in the depth of winter in mild areas. It is one of the best winter shrubs we have, easy as a rule and very hardy. Nobody seems to know exactly what soil it needs, but I have seen it flourish in very acid ones, so probably it is better without lime.

The flowers are followed by berries, white from white flowers, scarlet as a guardsman's jacket from the purple variety and birds love these and spread the seeds widely. This is strange because the berries – probably the seeds only – are extremely poisonous. Linnaeus claimed that six berries would kill a wolf, though how many wolves he saw come to an untimely end in this way is not known. He did say that he saw a girl die after taking twelve for an ague. Anyhow it was a risky plant to use for medicine. Gerard described 'the heate of his mouth, and choking in the throte' caused by eating one berry, and other writers on gardening all tell the same story. So Mezereon (the English form of the name) is rather strong meat. It must contain some potent drug or drugs, but they are better avoided – unless of course you have wolves about that you want to get rid of!

But as long as you are not competing in the drug market the commonest Daphnes are delightful in any garden.

D. blagayana is prostrate with scented cream-coloured flowers. *D. burkwoodii* grows into a bush some three feet high and the early summer flowers are pink and fragrant. The fragrance can be taken for granted in most members of the family. *D. cneorum* is useful as a rock garden shrub. The flowers are a good rose colour. *D. collina* is another for the rock garden. *D. odora* flowers in winter and is, as you would guess, strongly scented. It is said to be quite hardy, but there is a little doubt on this point so some winter protection is advisable. *D. pontica* is probably about the toughest of the tribe, apart from *D. laureola*, and will grow freely in cold heavy soils, even under trees which drip cold drips all over it. Not many shrubs flourish under trees, so it is worth a place.

The name is derived from Daphne that lovely nymph who was pursued by Apollo and turned into a Laurel by the gods so that she should escape him. What fun those ancient Greeks had in their love lives! Of course the name was a mistake. The Laurel was *Laurus nobilis*, the Bay, and the Daphne got the title because of the similarity of its leaves to Bay leaves.

DEUTZIA   When I first grew this shrub it was rather a Plain Jane. It was useful, it was reliable, and the small white flowers in early summer made a good show and as I had used it in a rather rough inhospitable corner (not in my present garden) it was very welcome. But it was hardly exciting nor could I claim it was a breath-taking beauty.

But the plant breeders have been at work on Deutzias and there are some very pretty garden hybrids coming along and the best are really worth growing.

I think my first specimen was *Deutzia scabra*, and it seems to have been the parent, or one of the parents, of many of the named varieties you will find in the nurseries and the catalogues. Size and colour of the individual flowers have been improved out of all knowledge and a 6-foot specimen of Perle Rose, almost completely covered with rose flowers in June, is really a sight to gladden any heart.

Most of the species came from China though a couple are natives of North America but on the whole the well-bred garden forms are the best for planting. Mont Rose is another pink, while Pride of Rochester is a variety of *D. scabra*. The flowers of Contraste are lilac, rich purple outside.

D. clunii, D. rosea, D. magnifica are all worth a place, or a choice of one is, but the development of this delightful, easy-to-grow shrub is so recent that almost any you choose is fairly certain to be worth having.

DIERVILLA   Botanists *must* be accurate in naming plants but when that has been admitted it must also be admitted that it is a bit hard on the poor old gardener who finds that something he has found under one name all his life is suddenly under another.

So with Diervilla. Some nurseries and books use that name. Others say 'see Weigela'. And vice versa. What *has* happened is that most Diervillas have been renamed Weigela. For all practical purposes they are the same: bushes about 3 or 4 feet tall that in early summer are covered with trumpet-shaped flowers usually scented. They are easy, flower freely, and should be included in any collection of shrubs. The two Diervillas left in the genus usually on sale are *D. lonicera* (they are related to Honeysuckle) and *D. sessilifolia*. The latter is rather a small shrub, but they both have yellow flowers, *D. lonicera* being the darker in colour.

DIPELTA *Dipelta floribunda* is so much like a Weigela that anyone could be forgiven for confusing the two and if room is limited it is doubtful if there is much reason for growing both. The flowers are fragrant and the fully grown plant is rather taller and has more girth than the Weigela. This could be one reason for including it or not including it.

D. yunnanensis is similar but cream-coloured.

ERICA (Bell Heather) The name has nothing to do with Eric or Erica but is said to be derived from the Greek *ereike*, to break, because it is claimed a medicine made from it was used to break the stone (in the kidneys?). I cannot find any herbal in which this use is recorded, so the derivation is suspect. The popular name undoubtedly comes from the heaths on which they usually grow.

The family is peculiar in that it is distributed in a north-south belt on the globe mainly from Africa to the north of Scandinavia. There was not much interest taken in them as garden plants in early days. It is strange that so beautiful and widely distributed a flower received hardly a mention from author or poet all through the centuries – even the Scottish poets do not seem to have been moved to praise it.

Interest was awakened by the introduction of South African species late in the eighteenth century. They are very striking plants with large and beautiful flowers, and they really did get gardeners worked up. The early introductions were grown at

Kew and presently plant collectors were at work searching out new kinds. In a few decades about 400 were grown though many probably were hybrids. The Empress Josephine had a famous collection, which she imported from England, and she had the help and advice of John Kennedy, an English gardener. They carried out their wars in a more gentlemanly manner in those days and did not let them interfere with an important civilised occupation like gardening!

These exotic Heathers from the Cape were not for the everyday gardener: they were rich men's flowers. All were tender, and all were difficult to cultivate. As time went on, of course, many more people grew them, they were even used, in their pots, in bedding-out schemes, but they never took kindly to the blow hot–blow cold changes of an English summer – and the even-wider variables of a Scotch or Welsh one. The fashion died: it lasted well over a century, which was a fair run for a shrub that needed so much care. But curiously, the growing of tender Heaths had led to the hardy ones being noticed and presently those had taken over almost completely. You can still buy some of the Cape Heathers at florists and a few nurseries, and it is still problematical how long they will last. But while they do they are certainly striking flowers. They are not for the shrub garden though.

Heathers are, as a rule, low-growing shrubs. There are tall heathers, up to some 10 feet tall, but they come from Southern Europe and all of those are tender to some degree and some would be useless except in gardens near the South Coast. They are plants mainly for lime-free soils. If your soil contains lime then you can have *Erica carnea*, the winter-flowering Heather, and it will thrive. There are *E. darleyensis*, also winter-flowering, and *E. mediterranea* which has light red flowers on a 4-foot bush. *E. terminalis* and *E. arborea* are worth a try.

Of the others, there is a great host. Over the years the species have been hybridised and any nurseryman who has a good collection will have 40 or 50 kinds from which to choose. This, except for the dedicated specialist, is rather a pity. The colours

range from pink to purple, so there is much repetition and some
seem to differ mainly in the name. On the other hand, a lot of
the garden varieties are much more brilliant than their parents.

The only Tree Heather that can be recommended as hardy is
the Corsican Heath, *E. terminalis* sometimes listed as *E. stricta*, and
even with that I would not offer a guarantee in cold districts. It
makes a 3 or 4 foot bush and has rose-coloured flowers in summer.
Other Tree Heathers are *E. arborea*, *E. lusitanica* and a hybrid of
those two known as *E. veitchii*. *E. australis* is the Spanish Heath.

E. carnea, the Winter Heather which I believe came from
Austria, has a vast variety of garden forms. King George (deep
pink) is a favourite; Queen Mary is red; Prince of Wales is rose
pink; Queen of Spain is another pink shade. They are not all
'royals' and James Backhouse is widely grown while Cecelia M.
Beale is a very good white variety.

W. Keble Martin illustrates five native Heathers and mentions
eight. The largest of the Bell Heathers is *E. ciliaris*. It is a chancy
business to give common names: for instance Mr Martin calls
this Ciliate Heath, but in one list I have it is Dorset Heath. Then
there are Cornish Heath and Irish Heath and some people (not
the botanists, of course, they stick to Latin and accuracy!) who
get in a right old tangle sorting out one from another.

Mr Martin's illustrations are *E. ciliaris*, the large Bell Heather;
E. cinerea, less densely packed with bells; *E. tetralix*, which I have
growing near me on the moors of mid-Wales and which I have
transplanted successfully into my garden; *E. vagans*, the Cornish
Heath tightly packed with small bells; and *E. hibernica*, which is
obviously Irish Heath.

Stick to these and their many hybrids and you cannot go far
wrong. Venture outside and I commend you to St Phocas, the
patron saint of gardening. He may be able to help you. I can't.

In the small or medium-sized garden you may grow your
Heathers when and how you will; few or many. Saving the
dislike of lime they are not difficult. They make excellent ground
cover; spreading mat-like and grown in this way they are good
companions for taller shrubs. I will not say nothing at all will

grow through their branches for they are loosely spaced but those mats of branches can be lifted easily, the competing weeds will then be pushed down when you let the Heathers fall and very few plants will survive under such a blanket.

The best arrangement is a Heather garden if you have the room. Large or small, this will give you pleasure – and colour if you choose carefully – the whole year through. Such a garden needs a little thought and some careful arrangement because it must never become formal, but there are dwarf Heathers and some not so dwarf and monotony can be avoided by the hardiest of the taller sorts and by the use of a few dwarf conifers which themselves, by the way, should be grouped and not pushed in singly every so often like soldiers standing guard.

There are some splendid Heather gardens on view from Edinburgh and Harrogate down to Wisley, and a few beauties in private gardens, too. They are worth studying.

The chief commercial use of Erica is for making briar pipes. The briar has nothing to do with the rose but is *la bruyère*, from *E. arborea*. The wood used is in the roots of old specimens and the manufacture of the pipes was, and I believe still is, an important local industry in parts of many of the south European countries.

Apart from that, Heathers like Ling have been more used by peasantry than in urban trades. Young shoots are food for many animals, hare and deer, rabbit and sheep and some of the moor-land birds eat them. Most of what I wrote of Ling could be said of Bell Heather.

The plants make good thatch and in some parts, notably in Scotland and Ireland, have been used on the roofs of cottages and barns for centuries. It is said to be very warm when tightly packed, but I have been told it can never be made watertight on its own (I believe straw and reed can) and needs an underlayer of timber. Now whether a Highland cotter, say a hundred years ago, could afford a roof of timber on which to lay his thatch is a debatable point. Which, however romantically you look at thatch, makes you think.

Cut or growing, it makes a good bed. You could imagine it

would be a bit spiky. Not the sort of bed a real princess would
enjoy, if you remember Hans Andersen's story of the Princess
and the pea. But it is springy and the bits you would expect to
stick into you bend over. That has been my experience. When I
was a boy my brother and I and my father spent weeks all the
summer camping by or near the sea in south Pembrokeshire.
Sometimes we slept in the boat my father had made and sometimes on the cliffs and the moors. There were neither Li-los nor
camp-beds then and a ground sheet on the Heather was all we
had. But we slept the sleep of the just and woke from it like the
proverbial lions – with an appetite to match. Maybe it is only a
romantic nostalgia but it seems there was a fragrance in the
crushed Heather that was more effective than all the spells of
Morpheus. Better, anyhow, than sleeping pills!

The other use for Heather was to make another sort of bed:
the 'sail' as they called it, or bed on which the great haystacks
and cornstacks were built. Those were never erected on the bare
ground. Nobody told me but I think the Heather (and Gorse
sometimes) admitted a little air under the rick, and since an
overheated rick could burst into fire at any moment a little
ventilation was important.

And one other use: the plant was used in the brewing of
Heather Ale. This legendary drink, as sweet as the nectar of the
gods and as strong as Samson's right arm, cannot now be made
because the secret recipe is lost. Briefly, the story, as told in a
poem, was that the last two Picts to know how to make it (a boy
and his father) were captured by the Danes. If they told their
secret they were spared.

The boy said aside to one of their captors, 'The old man will
kill me if I tell. Throw him over the cliff and I will.'

So they threw the father over the cliff.

Then the youth said, 'Now you can throw *me* over. He was the
last man to know the recipe and I was afraid he would tell it to
save his life.'

So they threw him over too.

A pity!

Now I love a good legend, but I think I know what lies behind this. Hops came into this country early in the sixteenth century and a right old fuss was made about them:

> Hops and turkeys, mackerel and beer
> Came to England all in one year.

Parliament was petitioned to stop the growing of 'a wicked weed that would spoil the taste of the drink and endanger the people.' Gerard warned that 'too many do cause bitternesse thereof and are ill for the head.'

Before the hops came people used various herbs to flavour the ale, different districts using different plants. What more natural in Scotland and such places than to use Heather: the young shoots it may have been, or the flowers or both. Good beer is easier to make than tea or coffee (and, within reason, more wholesome). It *should* be (brewers take note) malt, sugar and hops fermented in water. There is nothing to stop any brewer, commercial or amateur, experimenting with the best-flavoured parts of Heather plants instead of, or as well as, the hops.

We may yet taste Heather ale again.

Heather honey is known to most people and some like it best of all. But Gerard had a curious comment on that.

'Of these floures (Heather and Ling) the Bees do gather bad hony.' Turner, as already mentioned, called it 'naughty'.

ESCALLONIA These are evergreen shrubs; I know of only two deciduous species, *E. illinata* and *E. ingata*. Escallonias are mainly of medium height and size and bear pretty flowers, pink or white in summer and early autumn. They are not common but are occasionally seen in seaside gardens where they are most useful for windbreaks because they do not seem to mind the salt winds. It is doubtful if they would stand direct gales straight off the sea but in the gardens behind walls or with the least shelter they thrive.

Inland and far from the sea they are not widely grown. They are natives of South America mainly, so have a reputation for being tender. They may be, too, but in light soils they are not as tender as is believed. I had a nice little bush of *E. edinensis* in my previous garden – it may still be there – and it came through some notable mid-Wales Arctic winters without a sign of discomfort. It was, however, high on a slope and the soil was thin and dry to harshness.

Hybridising with the hardier species has led to the introduction of varieties that will stand at least some frost, but I think if my *E. edinensis* is anything to go by, that heavy soils could well be avoided, and though mine was starved because I knew no better a mulch of good compost or a handful of fertiliser does any shrub a power of good.

Escallonias are such pleasant shrubs that they deserve more attention from those who garden inland and farther north. There are some good species but so much breeding has gone on it is not easy to know species from hybrids so most growers choose from the host of hybrids. Many of them came from Irish nurseries. Any with Donard in the title came from the Donard Nurseries in County Down and you can hardly go wrong with them. Donard Beauty (red), Donard Seedling (pink), Slieve Donard (apple pink), would make a pleasant start. *E. illinata* is white and by repute hardier than most; *E. rubra pygmea* is dwarf; *E. ingramii* also is white and tall, up to 12 feet or so, and not dangerously tender.

Escallonias are splendid for hedges; being evergreen they are attractive the whole year through. They require little pruning; as they flower mainly on shoots one year old any cutting back should be done immediately after flowering.

Euonymous This is a large family of shrubs, big and small, deciduous and evergreen. Largely they are Europeans though there are some natives of Asia and America. We have one native, *Euonymous europaeus*, the Spindle Tree, which will apparently grow and thrive in any garden but which I have only seen wild on or near the chalky soil of the Downs. Spindle, like all the family, is grown for the lovely fruits, which have been compared to a bishop's mitre. They alone, when cropping well, would be a good recommendation to plant; as a bonus there are beautiful leaf tints in autumn. It is not a shrub of very good shape or form and can grow to tree size so it is not suitable for a small garden. It has a host of common names: Dog-wood (usually kept for Cornus), Peg-wood, Louseberry, Gaitre-tree (I have wondered could that have been Goitre-tree) and many more.

The commonest, Spindle, refers to the hardness of the wood. Evelyn, noting that, said it was used for bows for viols 'and the Inlayer uses it for its colour, and instrument-makers for toothing of organs and virginal keys, tooth-pickers &c . . . I also learn that three or four of the berries purge both by vomit and by siege, and the powder made of the berry, being baked, kills nits, and cures scurfy heads.' Evelyn also has a rather curious note that 'they were wont to scourge parricides with rods made of this shrub before they put them into the sack.'

You would hardly think that parricides* were common enough to need a special rod to beat them.

But other days, other ways!

Spindle had medicinal uses, but the berries are certainly poisonous and probably other parts are as well. Gerard said it was 'hurtful to all things' which was not accurate as the caterpillars of a certain moth feed on the leaves, and it is a host plant to the black aphis. But then aphides are like Mithridates, who fed on poisons so as to become resistant to them; often they seem positively to enjoy them. The origin of the Latin name has been widely guessed at but if the plant is as poisonous as it is thought to be, it may well have come from Euonyme, the Mother of the Furies.

There is a wide choice of species to choose from, but many are too large for gardens. *E. europaeus* is our native Spindle Tree but if you live in the south you may spare yourself the moderate sum the nursery will charge you for it: you can find plenty of specimens on the Downs and it is so widespread that I am sure nobody will grudge you a little one from the roadside (but not from a

* I thought Evelyn's Latin had failed him here but according to the Oxford English Dictionary it is the correct form, not patricide, though the latter is sometimes used.

farmer's hedge, I beg you!). And remember it will grow to a good size so be sure you have room for it. *E. japonica* is useful for hedges, and will grow practically anywhere. *E. radicans variegatus* is an attractive little shrub if you like variegated leaves. *C. alatus* is not so good as a berrying shrub but gives very fine leaf colour. It is one of the smaller kinds, about 6 feet tall. *E. yedoensis* is rather like our own Spindle but is said to bear an enormous crop of berries and the leaves colour well.

FORSYTHIA When you can cover nine daisies at once with your foot spring has arrived. Nice to know that because with our fickle climate it may be the only signal. The opening of the yellow Forsythia flowers on their bare stems is almost as reliable a sign. This is an excellent and beautiful shrub. It is found in most gardens, in roadside gardens by the hundred, or thousand, so that every journey by road in late April and early May becomes, in suburbs, an almost monotonous procession of the yellow flowers.

A very pleasant characteristic of Forsythia is that it will open its flowers indoors, so that in the dark days of late winter you may pick a bundle of bare twigs, or branches, and a few days in a warm room will see them in full flower.

It is the easiest of shrubs to grow, doing well almost anywhere, but in some years birds will attack, and presumably eat, the buds. I have had a couple of bushes practically stripped and since I have one bush growing on a post of the porch the whole sad story can be seen. They (I fancy it is largely sparrows) strip off the calyxes and drop them. Since there are no flower buds thrown down, presumably they have been eaten. This may happen when food is short, or there may be aphides wintering in the buds. I have not worked that one out.

The shrub came from China, Japan and Korea in the 1830s and 1840s but did not get into gardens until about 1850. You can find plenty of choice now in the nursery, and lots of hybrids which, in one way and another, are improvements on the original. *Forsythia suspensa* and *F. viridissima*, but mainly they are different rather than better. *F. suspensa* and closely related varieties are tall and the branches are 'suspensa', which you could translate as drooping. *F. viridissima* is erect and a little later in flower.

Some are a pale yellow, as pale as Primroses; others are as dark as Buttercups. The variety with the largest flowers is said to be Lynwood Variety. *F. ovata* is light in colour and earlier than most; *F. intermedia vitellina* has dark yellow flowers. Take your choice. Only one thing is certain: the one the man next door plants will be more desirable in *some* way. But you can raise new plants by the score from cuttings, so the Tenth Commandment need not be invoked too seriously.

I have always said 'For-sithia' (i as in *in*) but since the shrub commemorates William Forsyth, a famous eighteenth century gardener, it is probably 'For-sythia' (y as in *scythe*). It does not matter but some folks like to get these details correct.

Forsyth was Superintendent of the Royal Gardens of Kensington and St James's. A good gardener for sure, but he did blot his copybook a bit by offering a recipe for healing wounds in injured trees. It was a concoction of cow-dung, lime rubble, wood-ash and sand, mixed to a paste with soap-suds and urine. There is no evidence that he did not believe the stuff would work, but similar mixtures had been used before without much result. Anyhow he got £1,500 for the recipe, and some people thought he should have known better. The stuff was called Forsyth's Plaister; it does not appear to have ever been widely used, but, let's admit it, worse remedies have been introduced and used often enough since. It doesn't seem to have done any harm – and that can't be said of all the garden panaceas.

FUCHSIA This shrub is another that is familiar to pretty well every gardener in the land and even to those who are not of the brotherhood. Their pendulous flowers, in almost every shade of pink, purple and red, and lots of white, are generally to be seen dangling all summer long on pot plants and in greenhouses. They are not hardy, but in this they are variable for though anywhere north of the Thames they will be cut back to ground level by frosts they seldom fail to shoot up again in spring and give a good account of themselves. In gardens near the sea they are hardy all round the coast. That does not mean they are hardy everywhere at sea level, but you do find them in the most unexpected places and I am told there are as fine Fuchsia hedges in the Orkneys as there are in Cornwall. Where they do thrive outdoors a Fuchsia hedge is a joy all through the summer and making an informal hedge is a splendid way of growing them. A cheap way, too, for these are shrubs that seem to enjoy growing from cuttings, and they grow quickly. The species most commonly used is *Fuchsia magellanica*. Another is *F. riccartonii*, but it seems probable that the latter is a form of *F. magellanica*, if not the same plant.

Fuchsias were first brought to Europe by missionaries just before 1700 but the whole story is so complicated with introductions and reintroductions that it would be easy to get bogged down in it for a chapter. The best-known story has been told many times and like all good stories, such as Alfred and the Cakes and Lady Godiva, has been discredited. But in its main details (as with those two pretty legends) it is correct. Here are the bare bones of it.

A famous Hammersmith nurseryman called James Lee was walking down a Wapping street about the year 1790 and in a window he saw a Fuchsia unlike any he had ever seen before. He called at the house and asked the woman who lived there if she would sell it to him. She was not willing to do this because it had been a present from her sailor husband. In the end she agreed to part with it for eight guineas, a fine sum in 1790, and the promise of two plants propagated from it. Lee took the plant home and raised 300 new ones. He sold them at a guinea each. The story finishes, but presumably he rooted more cuttings and sold more plants.

I won't spoil that brief account by all the variations that have been suggested by the story-wreckers.

Like many another plant the Fuchsia had an uneventful history for many years but about 1850 it became popular and the sale of plants ran into countless thousands daily. They were grown in every conceivable size, shape and colour and the Fuchsia Show must have been an astonishing sight. But enough soon becomes too much, and by 1900 fickle public taste had turned to something else. It is said that the end came with the Great War when greenhouses were used for food, such as tomatoes, and many pleasant flowers were turned out.

Nowadays you could say the Fuchsia has slipped into place as a good and useful shrub though (in theory anyhow) there is a host too many to choose from still. In his excellent book on the family *Fuchsias for all Purposes*,* Thomas Thorne gives a catalogue of 'Species, Hybrids and Varieties'. It takes up 95 pages with about 20 to the page. Mr Thorne had *seen* all these, so somebody loves them above all else.

What should you choose and where can you buy? Frankly I don't know, but there are a few nurseries growing only, or mainly, these plants and through the Royal Horticultural Society it would be possible to find out who and where they are.

For the average gardener the average shrub nursery will have from a dozen to a score of the best varieties, and if you get hybrids such as Brilliant, Display, Elsa and Mrs Popple they will make a pleasant start.

For hedging get *F. magellanica*, *F. exoniensis* which has larger flowers, or *F. riccartonii*.

And Leonhardi Fuchs after whom the family was named? Well, he was quite a person in his own right. He was a herbalist and a doctor and a teacher of medicine at the University of Tubingen in the sixteenth century. He wrote a very fine herbal and is remembered for his doctoring at Auspach during an outbreak of the Plague in 1529. He was only 28 years old at the time. And he never saw a Fuchsia in his life.

GARRYA   Only one species of this evergreen is usually grown. It is *Garrya elliptica* and is noted for its long greenish catkins which are borne freely in autumn and stay on the plant all winter. These are on the male plant but nurseries can generally supply the female form, which bears clusters of black fruits.

Garrya is an easy shrub but has a reputation for being a little

* Collingridge, 1959.

on the tender side. This may be the case with young plants before they have become settled. Near a wall or in a sheltered position they give no trouble. In the open garden a little shelter is advisable to start with, and perhaps some bracken or straw thrown over in the coldest weather. *G. thuretii* is good in windy situations.

GENISTA It is a pity that the botanists could not have stretched a point and put this genus in with Cytisus, for so many species are similar to so many species of Broom – are even called Broom – that it is difficult for the majority of gardeners to tell them apart.

As with other Brooms, by whatever name they are given in books and lists, they are best grown from seed, and if they are raised in small pots root disturbance, which they are said to resent, can be avoided.

All the family are excellent in hot dry positions. There they last longer than in heavy soil. In fact I never find seedlings in, say, the rich Rose bed or the mixed border.

There is a suspicion, a vaguely held idea, that some of the Genistas are not quite as hardy as the Cytisus. I do not think there is much in that, but there is one, *Genista canariensis*, which you can buy from the florist rather than from the nursery and that is a very good pot plant for a cool greenhouse. It can spend the summer outside but will not stand frost.

Of the dozen or so Genistas that are easily obtained, the Mount Etna Broom, *G. aetnensis*, is the tallest. It grows to about 12 feet and the flowering branches droop, so it has something of the habit of a weeping shrub. It flowers very freely and is a grand sight when in full bloom. In spite of the name it is as hardy here as it is at home.

G. cinerea is seldom much over 8 feet but the growth habit is similar. It flowers in August when a lot of shrubs have finished. I have heard it recommended as a companion to the purple Buddleia and though I have not seen it in such company it sounds a very pleasant mixture of colour. *G. falcata*, not seen too often, is evergreen. *G. hispanica* is the Spanish Gorse, and though as prickly as a hedgehog is a true Genista and not a Gorse (Ulex),

D

though in colour and form Gorse again is very near in appearance and from a distance could be the same. The Spanish Gorse, in the hot dry soil that suits it, makes absolutely a mound of colour. It reaches only about 2 feet but its spread is considerably more. G. *sagitalis* is still more prostrate and can be used in the rock garden, or even in a paved garden.

G. *virgata* comes from Madeira but does not seem unduly tender so long as it is in the hot dry soil all the Brooms thrive in. It is similar to G. *cinerea* but seldom grows as high.

Genista is the one plant known by every child, if they have learned their history, for it was the Planta Genista that became the badge and the name of the Plantagenet family. How and why this should be so is not clear, but there are legends linking the plant with the family from the tenth century and Fulk the Black, who may have been the first to use the flower as a distinguishing badge on the battlefield. In England it appears to have come into use by the House of York in the struggle with Lancaster for the Crown, though the more popular White Rose and Red Rose are regarded as the family badges, the Planta Genista being used as a family surname, though quite a few of the great families managed without those.

In France, too, Genista does not pass without notice; St Louis founded an Order of Chivalry, L'Ordre du Genest, in about the easiest date in all history, 1234. It figures in heraldry; the seed pods were used as well as the flowers and there is a religious picture in the National Gallery showing Richard II on his knees. His necklace of Broom pods is distinct and unmistakable.

Our native G. *tinctoria*, the Dyers' Greenweed, was used as a dye though not so much for the yellow as, with wood, to give a colour known as Kendal Green. Flemish weavers are given credit for this but there is, indeed, nothing new under the sun for Pliny had recorded the fact centuries before: 'the Green-weedes' saith he, 'do growe to die clothes with.'

HALIMIOCISTUS This is often included in catalogues and books as a species, but as the name indicates it is a hybrid between Cistus and Halimium. It is very like a Cistus and there are two that are hardy enough for most gardens in the south; in the north also, perhaps, but only trial and error can prove that for certain. *Halimiocistus ingwersenii* is a free-flowering spreading shrub with white flowers. It comes from Portugal where it was discovered growing wild. *H. sahucii*, also wild, comes from France.

HAMAMELIS   This is the Witch Hazel, so spelled though probably it should be *wych* from the old English *wice*, meaning pliant. It is a winter-flowering shrub that is worthy of a place in every garden, though it is hardly seen in one in twenty. The first species was brought from Virginia early in the eighteenth century, where the Red Indians valued it very highly for its medicinal uses. This *Hamamelis virginiana* is not much grown now except as a stock on which to graft the more-popular garden species.

The best-known, indeed the best of the genus, is *H. mollis*, from China. For many years it was grown in a few gardens without attracting much attention. Kew had a specimen or specimens for twenty years without anyone taking much notice of it. (How many gems have they still got, wasting their sweetness on the desert air!) About the year 1900 it caught the eye of the Curator (it must surely have caught it many times). The scales, as to another person on a more famous occasion fell from his eyes and he suddenly realised that this Ugly Duckling was a Swan. I think there could have been only the one specimen for it was promptly cut up and every possible twig grafted, presumably on to *H. virginiana*. From then on its progress was steady, although, as I suggested above, it has not been as widely planted as it deserves to be.

In leaf, and to some extent in form, it is rather like our Hazel. It can grow large in time and shapeless too, so a little skilful shortening of shoots could be used to keep it compact. The leaves are almost indistinguishable from Hazel – you'd not call that a shapely bush either – and they colour gloriously in autumn. The yellow flowers of rather curiously-shaped petals begin to come out in December and continue to do so until March. They are not usually affected by bad weather and have a delicious fragrance.

There is a form, *pallida*, with lighter-coloured flowers. Also there are some sub-species of *H. japonica* which are good shrubs, though all tend to be lanky in form. But *H. mollis* would always be my first choice. One variety, Carmine Red, has reddish flowers. While the American plant was the one originally used in medicine, the witch-hazel sold at the chemists' is as a rule made from *H. japonica*.

HEBE   See *Veronica*.

HEDERA   It would be easy here to write 'This is Ivy' and leave it at that. It is difficult to decide what to say about this native climbing shrub. A lot of gardeners do not like it at all; a lot more take very little notice of it; house owners are afraid of it because someone has told them it will pull their houses down (it won't!). Queen Mary, I have heard, disliked it so much she would not allow any tree in her gardens to give it hospitality; it will lift the slates on roofs . . . and so on. But it is not entirely without friends. The birds love it. One wall of my house is entirely and thickly covered by it, and in it they nest so closely that the wall is almost a bird tenement. How many kinds of birds live there I do not know because I have a feeling birds prefer to think their homes go unnoticed so I do not pry too closely, but at various times there have been the nests of blackbirds, thrushes, robins, various tits, nuthatches and, judging by the company on the bird table, quite a few more. And we have seen a mouse come out and dine with the birds more than once, a fact worth remembering since they could enter the house through an open window, and get in more easily than, once established, we could get them out.

On the whole, within reason, Ivy is a useful shrub, and within its sombre limits a very handsome one. If you have an old wall it will hold it together: it supports ruins not demolishes them. The castle walls *without* Ivy are the ones that fall down. Undoubtedly ruins will last longer if the Ivy is removed and the walls pointed with good mortar. But the Ivy holds the walls up for nothing whereas the mortar and an army of builders to do the pointing will cost a fortune.

There are many ways, both useful and ornamental, in which Ivy can be used imaginatively in the garden. It is excellent ground cover anywhere. Waste ground under trees will look much better with a carpet of Ivy. In my own garden I felled a Pine out of a group growing in one corner. I wanted some Yule logs! I left about ten feet of trunk and the Ivy growing from the base has now covered it entirely so that it has become an Ivy bush rather than a Pine stump. This, like the Ivy-covered wall, has become a minor bird sanctuary and gives hospitality to many a nesting bird, hospitality which they repay all too often by eating my fruit. But they would come in and do that anyhow and you can't have everything.

There is a vast host of the Hederas, the common Ivy being *Hedera helix*. This in turn has another host of sub-species and varieties, large-leaved, small-leaved, crinkled, silver, golden and variegated. To most people Ivy is Ivy and nothing more, but looked at closely, either in the nurseries or in the woods and hedgerows, there is a lot of difference in them and the leaves of some are beautifully marked and coloured.

So if you are in doubt have a hard look at your garden and see if there is any place in which this most useful of plants can be planted. The one place I would not have it is on a roof; there it will certainly push through tiles or slates and I cannot see that the stems as they thicken will do any good at all.

In story, legend, folklore and herbal use the plant has a very prominent place. The Greek name for it was *Kissos* from which we get Bacchus because Bacchus was found under a bush of it. That was not a tale to satisfy curious Greek children; his mother, Semele, had abandoned him there. The leaves of Ivy figured in his garland, but they signified sobriety not intoxication. The Vine leaves represented that. Pliny said that the berries would prevent drunkenness. In many ways Ivy crept into an association with wine. It became the Bush in inn signs; the Ivy Bush is a common pub name. It was hung up as an inn sign ('Good wine needs no bush') and it was the sign hung over drinking booths at fairs for hundreds of years. Cups were made of the wood; both Culpeper and Evelyn noted that and there was a belief wine would soak through such cups but water would not. These cups had medicinal uses. 'Those that are troubled with the spleen shal find much ease by continual drinking out of a Cup made of Ivy, so as the drink may stand some small time therein before it be drunk.'

It had to take second place in decoration at Christmas though. 'The Holly and the Ivy,' goes the old carol. 'The Holly bears the crown.' But decoration is not everything. 'To dream of Ivy foretells friendship, happiness, good fortune, honour, riches and success.'

HIBISCUS The common name is Tree Mallow. It is rather neglected by gardeners which is a pity as it is a good shrub, very easy to grow and gives a good account of itself when in flower. An introduction from China and India, it appears to have been used in gardens as far back as we have records. It flowers quite late in the summer at a time when a lot of the shrubs have finished, and it often flowers late into the autumn. *Hibiscus syriacus* is the species to plant. Indeed, this in one of its many garden forms is the only one the nurseryman is likely to offer, for all the others, something like 150, are tender.

In most gardens *H. syriacus* is quite hardy, but it may be that in a few here and there, or in a cold or windy site, it may fail. John Parkinson, for instance, reported that it was tender and should in winter be 'kept in a large pot or tubbe in the house or in a warme cellar if you would have them thrive.' So when planting it is worth bearing in mind that it *might* be on the safe side to give it a warm position.

Colours vary; they are mainly in the blue-purple-red shades, and some whites and whites with coloured centres; the choice of varieties will differ from nursery to nursery. *H. syriacus coeleste* is a good blue. *H. syriacus rubis* is red and Snowdrift is white. Duc de Brabant is a double red and there are doubles in other shades.

The leaves have been used in the same way as tea in China and the flowers as food – possibly as salad, though they may have been cooked. I cannot find any recipes and my favourite Chinese restaurant is not very helpful, so perhaps, like Samphire in our country, a dish of Mallow leaves is a possible rather than a probable addition to a meal. The fruits and seeds of some of the tender species are edible and some have medicinal properties. Culpeper had a couple of pages listing its uses, which is good measure, even for him. 'Pliny saith, That whosoever shall take a spoonful of any of the Mallows, shal that day be free from al Diseases that may come unto him.'

HYDRANGEA The common Hydrangea is *Hydrangea hortensis*, of which there are as many named varieties as even the most enthusiastic grower could wish. But we are on delicate ground again. The actual plant, so far as my knowledge goes, is hardy anywhere; the flower buds are not. They are very susceptible to frost damage. The trouble is they seem to vary from garden to garden. In my own, and it was the same in my other garden a few miles away, bushes have grown well outside. I always gave them favoured spots in sunny corners or against south walls. But I never had a flower on them. Yet in other gardens within, say, half a mile, I know of fine specimens that blossom reliably year after year. To get flowers I have to grow them in large pots or tubs and bring them in for the winter. So I find it difficult to recommend Hydrangeas as outdoor subjects for cold districts or for any place subject to frosts and east winds. South of the Thames, yes; and in seaside gardens, but in them preferably out of the worst of the gales.

The best are never cheap so it may be worth giving one or two a trial run before you put in an avenue of them expecting a vista of white, pink or blue like that drive you saw on your holiday in Devon or Cornwall.

If you can flower them out of doors there are many ways they can be used and many places they can be useful as well as beautiful. For instance, they will grow in light shade. In south Pembrokeshire I have seen them used in woodland. We seldom had a hard winter there but now and then we got notable frosts. I remember I learned to skate on a flooded meadow one winter and more than once I have known the edge of the sea to freeze. But the

Hydrangeas seemed to thrive, though I cannot say whether they flowered in those years.

H. hortensis is sterile; that is, it does not set seeds. But cuttings taken in midsummer root so easily that it is a wonder anyone bothers to buy plants.

Colours are generally white and shades of pink. Some of the pink ones, *not* white, will come blue in soils free of lime. In lime-free soil some shades can be persuaded to turn blue by watering them with a 'blueing' compound. Watering with an alum solution is said to turn the flowers blue, but the blueness varies from good to purple-blue horrid. There used to be a yarn that plenty of rusty nails in the compost would do the trick, but for me it would not work. I have seen those Pembrokeshire Hydrangeas in their woodlands of such an intense rich blue that it would put a Mediterranean sky to shame, but I have also seen them in other places artificially blue, that reminded you only of chilly complexions on a cold winter day. A good blue is glorious, but if you can't manage a good one, then it is better to settle for a rich pink or a red. I wish I could explain these vagaries of colour but I cannot, though I believe it is a matter of minerals in the soil.

The florists' varieties are widely grown in greenhouses or as house plants, though they are really too large to be kept in rooms for long, and many people are surprised when they find there are other excellent species from which to choose. The genus as a whole tends to produce sterile flowers that are showy, or fertile flowers that are nothing much to look at. Some flowers bear both sterile and fertile flowers. The gardener must choose kinds that give at least a proportion of decorative flowers.

H. arborescens grandiflora is a good shrub, hardier than *H. hortensis* and a very useful substitute where the latter will not flower.

H. aspera macrophylla has naturally blue, sterile flowers and pinkish fertile ones, but it is not one of the easiest to grow. It is a good shrub for semi-shade and appears to do best in thin woodland.

H. paniculata has flowers not in the familiar mop or ball shape

but in pointed heads reminiscent of heads of Lilac. It can grow
very tall, so may need fairly hard pruning if room is restricted.

H. petiolaris, which you may find in the catalogue as *H.
scandens*, is the climbing Hydrangea. It climbs by means of aerial
roots, like Ivy – though, unlike Ivy, it is deciduous. It is perfectly
hardy, very vigorous, and the flat heads of bloom in early summer
have a good share of decorative sterile white flowers. It is a good
climber for shade, and as well as growing on walls will grow
happily on an old tree or anywhere it can find something on
which to cling.

HYPERICUM   The common name is St John's Wort and the plant
was associated with St John the Baptist. The most common
species is *Hypericum calycinum*, or Rose of Sharon.

'I am the Rose of Sharon and the Lily of the Valleys.' The
botanists are grand fellows and we could not do without them,
but they never did have any genius when it came to choosing
lovely names.

The Rose of Sharon is a beautiful shrub with many virtues and
one grave fault. The fault, of course, is that like many other
beauties she is too free with her favours. It will grow anywhere,
in sun or shade, in good soil or poor, in the baking sun or on a
cold windswept hillside. But it does spread – not uncontrollably
in gardens, where you can easily pull out all that overspills its
bounds. In the wild or where there is nothing to stop it it can
become overpowering. One species, *H. perforatum* (because the
devil bored holes in the leaves, hence *perforatum*, in trying to
destroy it) did become a real menace in Australia a century ago,
and it still is a nuisance, I hear, in parts of California. In my
garden there is a pretty little wild one, *H. pulchrum*, I think – a
lot of the wild ones are very similar except to botanists – but it
shows no sign of getting out of hand and when it appears in the
right places I leave it alone.

The shrub has been cultivated since the days of the Greek
herbalists at least. There is a story that *H. calycinum* was brought
from the Holy Land for its herbal uses by a north-country
Crusader. Like other legends that might well have a basis of

truth. As a garden plant it was introduced from Turkey about 1675. Other Hypericums had, however, been around long before that and many herbalists had sung their praises.

H. calycinum makes excellent ground cover, all the better for being evergreen, as most of the species are. It is gay all summer and far into autumn, with its golden flowers and brush of stamens from which it gets its second common name, Aaron's Beard. The fruit is less regarded but it is by no means insignificant.

H. dyeri from the Himalayas is about 3 feet high with much smaller flowers than calycinum.

H. frondosum. This is deciduous, about 4 feet, with the flowers in clusters. A very pleasant little bush.

H. patulum (or *H. forrestii*) is a good neat shrub, but the garden variety Hidcote is far better than the species, with larger flowers borne all through summer. If the dead blooms are pinched out every few weeks it hardly seems to flower less freely for months. Depending on position it becomes anything from 4 to 6 feet high. It can be pruned as you wish, hard or not at all; can be used as a hedge or as ground cover and is easily propagated from cuttings. It is in every way a first-rate shrub.

There is one more really valuable member of the family. This is Rowallane Hybrid, some say the finest of them all, but there is a little doubt as to its complete hardiness so it is wise to give it some shelter. In mild districts it grows 8 feet or more in height.

There are many native species of this plant though not all are shrubs. Mr Keble Martin, on whom I lean heavily for my botany, describes 21 and illustrates 16, but he includes *H. calycinum* which is almost certainly an escape from gardens, while others of his species, as I have mentioned, are so similar as to appear to the untrained eye to be the same.

So when we go back to the herbalists, who also were not always clever botanists, it is not clear sometimes about which they are talking. What *is* clear is that the Hypericums, taken collectively and regarded as one, were St John's Wort. It was valued highly both as a magic plant and as a source of medicine. It had power

over evil spirits; it protected people against lightning or demons
or witches or the Evil Eye. It was worn in the hat, in amulets,
strewn on the floor, laid under the pillow. Burton in *The Anatomy
of Melancholy* recommended it for depression and insanity.
Gerard said the oil from the flowers cured wounds. Evidently the
beliefs in its virtues were widespread: sixteenth century William
Turner called it Tutsan (*tout sain*) 'because it healeth all' while far
away in Spain Altisiodora used the juice to heal Don Quixote's
cat-scratched face.

Happy days, when simple people believed such simple magic.

We are wiser now. Or are we? I know a woman who only
lately paid a lot of good English guineas for a pot of some new
elixir of youth concocted by a famous Swiss doctor-chemist. It's
always a Swiss doctor – or a Swede!

ILEX We are back to the Ivy again – or nearly so. A pity that
Hedera and Ilex could not have come together, so closely are they
associated.

> The Holly and the Ivy
> When they are both full grown,
> Of all the trees that are in the wood,
> The Holly bears the crown.

In the plaintive music piped by the carol voices of children is
epitomised all the nostalgia of the Christmases of long ago.

There are so many Hollies that it is difficult to select. A nursery
may offer up to 40 or so species and garden varieties, though
except for hedging few gardens would have room for more than
a few of them.

There are Hollies with the familiar dark green spiny leaves;
Hollies with few or even no prickles. Some have gold leaves,
some silver, some variegated. Some trees have berries, others
none, while some have yellow ones instead of the familiar scarlet.
Ilex ferox is the Hedgehog Holly with enough spines to justify
the comparison with that prickly gentleman. There are small
Hollies while some are almost forest trees. The list could be
continued.

Luckily, the Common Holly, *Ilex aquifolia*, is well enough known to need no detailed description and, taking everything into consideration, the Common Holly is the most useful for the Common Garden.

It will grow almost anywhere, but, naturally, the better the soil and situation the better your tree will be. Hollies do not transplant very easily. The soil should be reasonably warm (May or October) and it is most important to guard against cold drying winds at the time of transplanting and also against loss of too much moisture through the leaves by watering and, if necessary, covering with damp sacks.

The other important point to watch is that you get a specimen that will bear berries. Holly is dioecious, that is, male flowers and female flowers are borne on different trees, though some have flowers of both sexes. I have one good tree and as there is no other near it and it has good crops of berries it must bear both male and female flowers. But this point needs watching – otherwise, no berries, and what is a Holly without berries!

Propagation is by cuttings, which is slow and uncertain, or by seeds which is slow and certain. The birds – I take it to be the birds – spread the seeds everywhere in my garden and seedlings come up in the most unexpected places.

One really good Holly tree is as much as most gardeners will want to spare room for. But it is an excellent hedging plant and John Evelyn's famous Holly hedge at Saye's Court was, he *said* (gardeners have been known to exaggerate!) 'four hundred feet in length, nine feet high and five in diameter' (through). This was mentioned earlier. He let his house to Peter the Great and Peter used to get a servant to wheel him in a barrow through the 'impregnable' hedge. I cannot find that Evelyn actually tells this tale in so many words, but he writes of the hedge and then mentions 'my now ruined gardens at Saye's Court (thanks to the Czar of Muscovy)'. In fact, I do not know where the story originated, though I have seen a picture of Czar Peter having his wheelbarrow ride. Perhaps, as with so many a good story somebody made it up. Just after the passage quoted above Evelyn writes of his hedge: 'It mocks the rudest assaults of the weather, beasts or hedge-breaker.'

But not an Emperor in a wheelbarrow?

Curiouser and curiouser, as Alice said.

Evelyn gave a very full recipe for making birdlime from Holly. Perhaps the less said of that the better. He records a multitude of uses for the timber, from inlaying to 'even hinges and hooks to serve instead of iron.'

All the herbalists recommended it for one ointment or another, though not always for the same ailment. Evelyn added his quota which included 'a dozen of the mature berries, being swallowed, purge phlegm without danger' and a posset of the most pointed leaves in milk or beer was good for assuaging the torment of the cholic, when nothing else prevailed.'

JASMINUM A good many of the Jasmines do manage to be self-supporting but the best of them are trailing shrubs that are used as climbers. They can, however, if grown against a wall, be allowed to sprawl forward and then in time they will form a mound-like shape, quite a symmetrical one too, that is very pleasant and not at all untidy or formless.

Many of the species are slightly tender and in cold places can fail even with wall shelter. These should be used as greenhouse climbers. *Jasminum polyanthum* for instance is so delightfully scented that it is a shame to be without it. This species and the equally fragrant *J. primulinum* usually survive the rigours of a winter in Torquay or Bournemouth, but I would not give much for their chances on the Yorkshire Moors. *J. officinale* is the one most often grown outside but it has been known to fail, and in not very northerly places at that. It is a dainty thing but not so substantial or as strongly scented as the two tender ones mentioned. Not everyone wants the heady perfume, of course. Gilbert White of Selborne thought it a bit much: 'the jasmine is so sweet that I am obliged to leave my chamber.'

There are other Jasmines, not common and, really, in view of their doubtful hardiness, not very useful, but any gardener with a genial climate at his service and a love for delicate scented flowers would enjoy growing some. Those most easy to obtain are *J. beesianum*, *J. diversifolium*, which is a choice Himalayan species, *J. geraldii* and *J. stephanense*.

The most useful, certainly the best-known is *J. nudiflorum*, the winter-flowering Jasmine. This is one of the most useful flowering shrubs we have. It has deep yellow, unscented Primrose-shaped flowers on long trailing stems from November to March. The unopened buds are strongly tinted with red. The plant is completely hardy; the flowers, sad to say, are not and hard frost ruins them. But each twig bears a succession of them so if you lose some a fresh lot soon appears. Given the shelter of a warm wall they are fairly reliable if hard frosts can be dodged and a mound-like bush spraying out under a south-facing window is a cheerful sight indeed on a dreary December or January day. Sometimes a specimen is seen spread over a wall and tied in, but I think a better show is achieved by supporting only a few low branches and then allowing the bush to grow naturally.

This is the best easy flower I know for giving cut flowers the whole winter through. We gather great bunches of the long bare stems, put them in water in the house and in a few days' time they are in full bloom. Perhaps it is just as well they are not scented. They could easily be overpowering if they were and then we should be without our unfailing winter flower supply.

Winter-flowering Jasmine is easy to propagate from cuttings, but the trailing shoots root freely as they go, so a well-grown specimen will always have plenty of its offspring on its skirts all ready to transplant.

Jasmines have been known to gardeners for so long that the origin of the older species is not known. Obviously it was in warmer eastern countries, and most of those we grow out of roughly 200 species came from parts of Asia from Persia to China. They have been used in medicines: 'The oile which is made of the flowers hereof wasteth away raw humours, and is good against cold rheums.' But Gerard, who wrote that, also warned 'the overmuch smell thereof maketh the nose to bleed.'

Its chief use has been in perfumery and the manufacture of

various pleasant-smelling toilet aids; for these it has been highly valued since the times of the ancient Greeks and probably long before them. As Evelyn said, 'we will leave that to the Chemist and the Ladies, who are worthy the secret.'

The name of the flower does seem to have got into the fringes of our vocabulary. Jessamy gloves were scented with the flowers. Then there was Oliver Goldsmith's 'jessamy bride' (Mary Horneck) and the Jemmy Jessamy adorers mentioned by Thackeray in *Barry Lyndon*.

KALMIA The Kalmia is hardly a common shrub in gardens, though in a lime-free soil such as suits Heathers and Rhododendrons it is not difficult to grow. Where and when it does thrive it is one of the loveliest of shrubs for late spring or early summer. It needs a peaty type of soil, a cool site and ample moisture, though not, I think, a wet stagnant position. Three species are commonly grown. They are all evergreen and the best is *Kalmia latifolia*. This is very similar in appearance to a Rhododendron. It will reach some 5 feet in height. The blooms, which appear in June, are in flattish heads of small flowers, pink in colour, the shade varying a little in seedlings. A form called *K. latifolia myrtifolia* is smaller, about 3 feet, more compact and perhaps would be more suitable than the parent species for small gardens.

K. augustifolia is another 3-foot species, generally deeper in colour, while *K. glauca* (or *K. polyfolia*) is smaller still, up to 2 feet, and might do for background in a rock garden. The flowers of this are rose-purple. This species, grown where it is suited, spreads by means of suckers which can be taken off to provide new plants.

These shrubs have no popular common name, though *K. latifolia* has been known as Mountain Laurel, Spoonwood, because Red Indians used to make spoons from the roots, and Calico Bush. Perhaps the name Kalmia is best, for the botanist Kalm in honour of whom Linnaeus gave it its name seems to have been a very pleasant and modest man.

K. augustifolia was sometimes called Sheep Laurel, not because sheep liked it, though apparently some did, but because it was poisonous to them. All the species appear to be poisonous, more or less, and there is a belief that the flesh of partridges that have fed on the berries is not to be trusted. Also honey made from the nectar of the flowers is said to be poisonous, so Kalmia is hardly a shrub for bee-keepers' gardens. I have read that where *K. augustifolia* and *K. latifolia* grow wild the bee-masters try the honey on dogs before letting human beings eat it. Hard luck on the dog, and it seems a rather primitive way of testing for poison. It is curious that unwholesome honey comes only, as far as I can learn, from the plants that need lime-free soil. There was the Azalea honey that upset the digestions of Xenophon's Ten Thousand – that is an old story indeed – and though many people prefer Heather honey to any other, some say it makes them ill. There surely must be some link between the iron in certain soils and the unwholesome elements (or compounds) that get into the flowers of the plants which flourish in those soils.

Some clever chemist might like to work out that one!

KERRIA There is only one species of this shrub. It is *Kerria japonica* and it is Japanese though it reached us in 1805 from China. There are three varieties available. *K. japonica* itself has single flowers like large buttercups. This is rarely seen in gardens, the double form, *K. japonica flore-pleno* being the popular one, and *K. japonica picta* a variegated form of that. It used to be known as Jews' Mallow because it was confused with another plant, the leaves of which were supposed to be a popular ingredient in Jewish salads. The most usual common name is, and always was, Gypsy Rose. It was a great favourite in cottage gardens, probably because it is so easy to grow that it could be given away freely. It is very, very easy, very pretty and though single specimens would be rather formless small thickets of the stiff stems make a pleasant sight in corners and difficult sites. It spreads rather too easily, but unwelcome wanderers are no trouble to pull out and, like unwanted kittens, generally can be placed in good homes. Though it was such a popular cottage garden shrub years ago it is by no means as common as it was and certainly not as common as it deserves to be.

LAURUS *Laurus nobilis* is the true Laurel of classical fame. It is commonly known as Bay. It is as well to clear up this point tidily, but alas, gardeners are apt to be stubborn about names they have used all their lives, and their fathers before them, so presumably we shall all go on using the wrong labels for a long time to come, while the botanists weep over our sins.

Briefly, what we commonly call Laurel is a member of the Plum family and its correct name is *Prunus*. We shall come to that all in good time.

The true Laurel, only one species being grown, is *L. nobilis* or, as already mentioned, Bay; the green Bay Tree of the Psalmist, which incidentally *does* flourish in Mediterranean countries, where it grows into a large flowering tree.

The classical fairy-tale about it is that Apollo fell in love with the nymph Daphne. It would seem that the feeling was not mutual for she ran away, in the manner of those happy, free-for-all days when love or no love depended on which of two people could run the faster. Apollo pursued her. She called to her father the river-god Peneus to help her and he turned her into this tree. Apollo made it sacred to himself and the leaves became the victor's laurels, the poets' bays, the crown of athletes. All kinds of lore and legend accumulated round the tree, a common one from the time of Tiberius to Culpeper being that it was a protection against lightning, Culpeper including devils and witches: 'neither witch nor devil, thunder or lightning, will hurt a man where a Bay tree is.'

'So much might be said of this one tree . . . from the cradle to the grave we have still use of it, we have still need of it.'

Every herbalist had some favourite recipe. Wasp and bee stings and coughs; to 'weish out freckles,' said William Turner. It was 'good for a cold liver, dronk in strong wine,' said Gerard: for 'cold griefs in the joints,' said Parkinson; Evelyn thought it would cure agues and also recommended the wood for strong staves for Old Gentlemen.

Out of these what chiefly remains is a flavouring for the cook. It is a pleasant flavour – within reason. Too many cooks forget that too much herb destroys the flavour of what is being cooked. Strong herb flavours were better than those of badly salted meat in the days when there was little fresh meat in winter. That is why our ancestors used herbs so freely.

Bay is a good shrub outside in the warmer parts of this country, but may be better for a little protection where the winter is long and cold. It is useful as a specimen tree for a tub, where it is just as pleasant grown naturally as clipped into some odd shape.

LAVENDULA The name is near enough to Lavender to be easily recognisable. Widely grown and greatly loved this dwarf shrub seems to be most typical of English plants. Yet Old English Lavender is not as English as all that and there is no reference to it that I know of earlier than about the middle of the sixteenth century. It grows wild in most Mediterranean countries and I have seen it growing wild quite high in the Pyrenees. The name is from *lavare*, to wash, and the Romans used it to perfume their baths and washing water. Since they bathed here as freely as they did at home I think they must have introduced it. But why the neglect between the Romans and the sixteenth century? Though there are many records of what was grown in some monastic gardens in medieval times there is no mention that I have ever seen of Lavender. Garlic, onions, leeks, fennel, yes:

> 'Percely, clary and eke sage
> And all other herbage.'

But no word of Lavender. Strange! You could hardly overlook it and it has not lacked friends. You never hear anyone say he dislikes this most scented of plants.

There are many ways of growing it: as single bushes, as an edging plant, as low hedges, loose and straggling or neatly clipped; as a background shrub in the rock garden, where it has every right to be. I have tried it as ground cover but this was not a success. It does not hug the ground enough, its natural habit is far too loose and the grass treats it with no respect, will grow through it and almost over it. But it is a splendid little bush for a tub or other container on a sunny warm porch or a paved garden.

There are not many species. Three are commonly available. *Lavendula spica* is the Old English Lavender and was probably the early kind that helped to make Shakespeare's Bucklersbury so pleasant. Bucklersbury was the Tudor herb market: 'smelling as sweet as Bucklersbury in simpling time.' Presently Lavender was being grown in the nursery gardens around London and it features in the Cries of London and there can hardly be anyone not familiar with the picture of the pretty Lavender Girl on the bottles of perfume and toilet aids, which I think comes from an old print.

'Buy my sweet Lavender.' I expect they did, too. London street odours must have been a strong-smelling pot-pourri at times and something pleasant in the nostrils cannot have come amiss. The cities no longer smell of sun-warmed sewage, but why did they ever stop selling Lavender?: diesel fumes are not much better than sewage!

L. spica will reach 3 feet or more; *L. stoechas* is about 2 feet and *L. vera* is the dwarfest of all. In between there are a few garden forms, but this is a shrub without a great deal of variety. The leaves are more grey or less grey, the purple spikes of flowers light or deep in shade. There is a white kind, *L. nana alba*.

It grows easily from seed. In my early days when my wants were greater than my purse (I've suffered from that disability *since* my early days, mind!) I raised lots of plants from a packet of seed which cost only a few coppers. I had so many that I made a hedge of them. In my present garden I grew a hedge from cuttings and a very fine one it was and unlike my boasting fishermen friends I have a photograph to show I tell the truth. But beware where you grow a Lavender hedge. This one I made in front of the Roses and with the hedge in full flower you could not see the Roses behind: the dwarf ones, some of the Poulsen family I seem to remember, were completely hidden. It was Roses *or* Lavender: the Roses won and my lovely Lavender had to go elsewhere.

In general, apart from the extraction of the oil, it appears to have been grown for pleasure more than for use. It would hardly have been used in cooking – too strong for that; a pleasant smell does not necessarily mean a pleasant taste, but Lavender-flavoured cachous are common enough. I'm old enough to remember that women who were abandoned enough to smoke used to chew lots of them so that the neighbours did not smell out their wicked secret. A digestive medicine was once brewed from it, also a nerve medicine. 'A comfort to the braine,' said Turner, and that sums it up pretty well.

LIGUSTRUM   This is Privet and it can hardly be called a notable flowering shrub, though it does have flowers, of course, and quite pretty, though poisonous, berries.

It is rather in the doldrums at present. It grows everywhere so easily and so well, and has been used for so many hedges everywhere that many gardeners have come to despise it. We do not value what we get too easily. Yet it should not be despised, it still makes a very fine hedge; a few bushes are excellent for an odd corner and you could have a worse screen for some unsightly spot than a little group of Privet. It makes a good, quickly grown wind shelter. A bush of Golden Privet is as bright as a flowering shrub and can brighten the garden on many a dull day.

The species most used for hedges is *Ligustrum ovalifolium;* the variegated form is *L. ovalifolium auro-marginatum*, but it is easier to ask for Golden Privet and any shrub merchant will know what that is. *L. lucidum*, a Chinese species, is probably the handsomest of the family but it is not for small gardens as it can grow to tree size. If you have an old Lilac don't be surprised if you find Privet growing around it. It used to be nursery practice to bud Lilac on Privet, which was not really wise since Privet suckers readily.

LONICERA   With Honeysuckle we are back to the scented shrubs, and with a traditional British shrub at that. Some writers have cast doubts on the fact, Richard Jeffries for one, but there are species native to all parts of Europe, as well as Asia and America, so why should we have been left out? There are records of its being grown in thirteenth century gardens, and many authors, from Chaucer on, mentioned Woodbine at one time or another though that name has been variable. The present common name has been used for other plants; Clover was once called 'hunni-succles'.

There are bush Honeysuckles as well as the climbing kinds. Not all are of equal merit, though goodness knows enough are available to confuse a gardener who wants not a collection but merely one or two of the best.

Lonicera periclymenum is our native. It is variable because in woods and hedges so many have grown from seed. In scent there is not much to choose but the cross-pollination and seeding has resulted in differences in colour shades and size of bloom. The plants that grow in a hedge in my garden I take to be seedlings and the flowers are smaller and in smaller heads than some in a neighbouring wood. In the nursery they have heads of almost red flowers on the Late Dutch, which is *L. periclymenum serotina*. This is a splendid one to plant but an observant walker could very likely find equally good forms in many of our lanes.

L. brownii fuchsioides is another richly-coloured one sometimes called Scarlet Trumpet Honeysuckle. *L. americana* is more yellow and *L. caprifolum* Early Cream, is a good choice if you want a white one. *L. sempervirens* is the best of the evergreen ones, but the true species seems difficult to get hold of, although every nursery will have some variety. It has a reputation for being not quite hardy but on a south wall in my cold climate there have been no casualties though a very severe frost will often brown off a few of the leaves.

L. japonica is seen more in garden varieties than as the true species. It is good, reliable and grows quickly. This also is ever-green and is about the best choice where an unsightly building has to be covered in the shortest possible time. There is a form with variegated leaves but Honeysuckle is surely one plant better clad in its natural green. I do not think the flowers call for competition from the leaves.

Of the shrub species the best known and the most widely grown is *L. nitida*. It seems no time at all (it is though!) since it was being widely planted as a hedging shrub, and a very good hedge it made in a remarkably short time. But like Privet it was too generous and too easy, so now hardly anybody wants it. It has really very few faults as a hedge except that since it grows quickly it needs a trim with the shears occasionally. It roots so easily from cuttings that it will give you a hedge for almost nothing. Buy one plant in autumn, break it down into cuttings, stick them in and there you are – instant hedge!

The shrubby Honeysuckles are much less showy than the climbers but the sweet scent is there. On the whole they are not widely planted but *L. pyrenaica* and *L. tartarica* are pleasant little bushes. The most valuable in this group are the winter-flowering Honeysuckles. *L. purpusii* (a hybrid really) is about the best of these, the others being *L. fragrantissima* and *L. standishii*. The former is my favourite because my father had a huge bush in his garden and it became a sort of family custom to hunt out a few flowers on the way home from church on Christmas morning. They were few and tiny but the scent was very strong and, at a time of few flowers, they were very pleasant in a little vase in the house.

A shrub is a shrub. Not an original remark of course and with even less meaning than originality! But a shrub or any familiar plant is more than just a shrub, or plant. It is a word, a meaning, a proverb, a part of folklore, fairy-tale, even history at times. Our vocabulary would be less rich without them, our talk less colourful. On the whole honey has stolen the credit for sweetness from Honeysuckle; but the links with sweetness that twine itself about you is always there: 'Honesuckles, ripened by the sun, forbid the sun to enter.' Dr Johnson's reference to 'honeysuckle wines' was not kindly meant. The Music Hall song 'You are my honeysuckle, I am the bee,' was miles out. Bees cannot gather the nectar; that is done by Hawk Moths with their long tongues, if tongues is the right word, so really the plant is not very well named, for we get no honey from it.

But who cares? Poetry before accuracy.

Strangely, for such a fragrant, beloved plant, it was not much used in medicine. It was used for 'hitchcoughe or yisking' (hiccough?) according to Turner, and Gerard said the flowers steeped in oil and set in the Sun, are good to annoint the body that is benummed, and grown very cold.'

On the whole Honeysuckle was valued for its own sweet sake rather than for the uses that could be made of it.

LUPINUS The Tree Lupin, *Lupinus arboreus*, is a native of California where, I have been told, it can be seen covering wide tracts of hot hillside. In full bloom the mass of 4 to 6 feet shrubs is said to be a magnificent sight and the Sun draws the sweet fragrance out of the flowers, so that it perfumes the air all around.

It is not planted in this country nearly as much as it deserves to be, largely because of an imperfect knowledge of its needs. It is not a long-lived plant – flowering freely for a few summers then, after the manner of old soldiers, to gently fade away. But it is very easy to raise from seeds and where it is suited will often seed itself. Young bushes grow quickly so there is no long wait for blossom. The flowers are white or cream, often with a hint of purple. It thrives in hot dry positions in full sun and does better in soil which is a bit on the hungry side than in rich loam in which I have not found it as long lived as in harsh sunbaked stuff.

Named varieties are available but this is a shrub that gives good results from a packet of seeds. It is a good plan to raise the first batch of seedlings individually in small pots. Large specimens do not always move well.

MAGNOLIA This is one of the most beautiful of flowering shrubs and many gardeners have ambitions to grow one or two. But they are not exactly common and the reason may be that they are thought to be difficult. Another common idea is that they take years to reach flowering size. Neither belief is correct. They do grow the better and the faster for soil preparation and care at planting time but that is true of many other shrubs which are common enough.

A few species are slightly tender and are better avoided except in the mild south and south-west. Among these are *Magnolia campbelli*, and *M. delavayi* which has enormous leaves and flowers. Out of the 30 or so species and varieties likely to be on sale a few others are better left out of the average garden because they grow to tree size. *M. grandiflora* is notably in this class. I have seen magnificent specimens but much too large to be considered as shrubs. The flowers are lovely but they can be up to 9 or 10 inches across and that, in a small space, may look rather much.

Many of the genus flower early in the year. My own *M. soulangeana* has flowers before the leaves, which I suppose is its habit, though I have seen the same species on which the leaves have caught up the blooms. *M. soulangeana* is about the most widely planted. A pity, perhaps, because in cold districts the flowers are an easy prey to the March–April frosts which neither buds nor flowers seem able to withstand. *M. stellata* is a smaller shrub, equally charming, but again the flowers are too early for some gardens.

If I had room for only one I would plant either *M. sieboldii* or *M. sinensis*. They are summer-flowering and are more reliable than the early species. Both have white cup-shaped flowers, purple-stained on the outside. The Yulan, *M. denudata*, is lovely but the Yulan flowers early, also it grows rather large. As a lawn specimen in a warm southern garden it is good enough to deserve a trial. *M. lenei* is rather like *M. soulangeana* and may be a form of it, so unless you are collecting do not plant both.

M. watsonii is June flowering and handsome but inclines to tree-like proportions; *M. wilsonii* is similar and there is a hybrid of the latter that is claimed to be better. Almost any site will suit the summer-flowering kinds, though so many come from eastern Asia they may appreciate warmth. That is no rule. Parts of eastern Asia can be more than just chilly. The spring-flowering ones like sunny walls in cool districts and light woodland in warm ones.

Pruning might be mentioned here because wall specimens can grow so freely as to be overpowering. Some gardeners think that these aristocratic beauties will not tolerate too much familiarity from the pruning knife. The idea is unfounded. I put in *M. soulangeana* by a wall near a large window. The idea was that on cold spring days we should stand in the warm room and admire the flowers outside it. Very nice as far as it went but the tree grew so well that it threatened, when in leaf, to cut the light out altogether. I preferred light inside the room to a shrub outside so I cut off and I continue to cut off every branch and shoot that pushes across a pane. To balance, I cut off every branch pushing round the corner outside. The only result so far seems to be that we get more flowers (frost allowing) in a narrower compass. I also cut back over-tall shoots to keep a good shape. This is drastic treatment for such an aristocrat, but it makes me think that nobody need worry about pruning.

As for soil, Magnolias like a good, deep, well-cultivated loam. They benefit from peat, leafmould, compost and rotted manure, mainly when preparing the site. As long as it grows well do not overfeed your Magnolia. Anything more than peat as a dressing on a healthy specimen and you may well find yourself with a vigorous tree on your hands.

Nobody seems sure about lime. A few, *M. highdownensis* and *M. kobus* for instance, will tolerate it, and in Winchester, which is pretty near the chalk, I have seen some grand specimens of *M. soulangeana*. But as a piece of general, safety-first advice I would say, no lime.

In his book *A Chalk Garden* Sir Frederick Stern reports on the species he grew with success. They were *M. delavayi*, *M. kobus*, *M. sinensis*, *M. wilsonii* and *M. highdownensis*. If you have a lime soil any of these might be worth trying.

Magnolias of one sort or another have been known to European gardeners since the sixteenth century explorers began their journey to the New World. Another century and there were some in English gardens though, as might be expected, in the average garden they were rare or absent. For most people they were unobtainable and when a nursery did get hold of a few they were expensive. A number of travellers saw them and praised them. William Cobbett expressed the hope that some day they would be as common as Lilac in English gardens, a wish that has not exactly been granted, but easily could be. The Yulan was the first of the Chinese species to arrive. Sir Joseph Banks introduced it about 1790, though I think the exact year is not known. In China it had been in cultivation for about a thousand years, often as a dwarfed pot-plant for indoor decoration.

Strange that so striking a shrub has not gathered much folklore and superstition around it. Perhaps it has, but if so the stories have not travelled. Red Indians said you would die if you slept under it – while in flower, I presume – but whether anyone has tried the experiment I do not know. All countries have similar super-stitions: both Evelyn and Gerard have horror stories about sleeping under Yews, while in many parts of Asia it was the Upas Tree.

But the British climate does not tempt us to sleep under trees. MAHONIA   This shrub started off as a Berberis; indeed in many a botany-ignorant country garden it is still so called. It has now been placed in a genus of its own and that is fair enough because however closely related it is very definitely different in appearance. The first species to be grown here came from America between 1820 and 1830. It was known as the Oregon Grape and was edible. This was *Mahonia aquifolium* and it was very expensive, about £10 a plant. Many a gardener must have wished the price had held, for it seeds and suckers itself so freely he could soon have made a fortune. Later species arrived from the Far East. All are evergreen. They make lovely specimen shrubs, can be grown in groups, and are useful for hedges. They are ornamental at all seasons: in flower or with the berries on and most have lovely leaf colour in autumn.

Of the dozen or so species usually offered the most striking is *M. lomariifolia* from Formosa and Yunnan, but sad to say this one has a reputation for being tender except in mild districts. It has very long pinnate leaves (pinnate leaves are in pairs on a stem, like Ash leaves) and grand spikes of deep yellow flowers, Hillier's catalogue says as many as 250 to a spike; I take their word for it, I haven't counted. I have the feeling that somehow it does not fit in comfortably against a wall, but if your garden is cold in winter better perhaps have it somewhere than not have it at all.

M. aquifolium is holly-leafed, rich yellow in flower with black berries to follow. From the gardener's point of view it is a grand shrub to grow, for the early spring flowers, if cut, drop a shower of petals, stamens and pollen, so it escapes the shears of wicked marauding women. Leaf colour is good and as the whole plant is on the small side it is best to plant a group. It is easy to grow from seed, and as a rule will seed itself.

M. japonica. This is a choice shrub with fine pinnate leaves and lemon-yellow flowers. It is said to flower during the winter in mild districts, but so many districts are not mild. Early spring, very early in a good season, is the best most of us can hope for.

Those, for me, are the pick of the family. Of the others a few are slightly temperamental in cold places, though seldom to the point of dying in winter. Still it is well to choose carefully. The following are suspect: *M. haematocarpa* from Mexico, *M. nevinii* from California (those two are similar) and *M. pinnata* which some say is the most handsome of the tribe. *M. repens* is the Creeping Barberry and is useful for ground cover. *M. bealei* is similar to *M. japonica* and may be a variety of that species.

MALUS   Here is a tree that can be regarded as a flowering shrub as long as you keep to the smaller kinds. It was, if you believe in the Scriptures, grown right at the beginning of the world. 'She . . . took of the fruit thereof, and did eat, and gave also to her husband with her and he did eat.'

And who, pray, said it was an Apple? The Bible? Indeed, no! 'The fruit of the tree', Genesis tells us. The Mohammedan Scriptures? They are vague; in fact the Mohammedan guess is the grape or the fig. There must have been a first time when the fruit of the Tree of Knowledge was named as the Apple, but nobody seems to know when it was or who named it.

Cultivated Apples have been grown in this country since the Romans were here but it is almost certain that the wild types or crabs are native trees since they grew all over Europe. As orna-mental garden shrubs and small trees the accent in modern gardening is on the various smaller species and varieties of Crab Apple, but there is no doubt whatever that the fruiting types are as ornamental in flower and in fruit as any of the wild ones. I know one gardener who had no room in his garden for Apple trees so he planted them in his borders. He bought the ones grafted on dwarfing stock, keeps them a reasonable size by pruning new wood fairly hard and so gets the best of two worlds; shrubs beautiful in flower and fruit – *and* fruit that is edible. This sounds a bit unconventional but it is no new idea. The old country gardens, not only the cottage ones, but also those of big houses, even mansions, grew their Apples among the shrubs and flowers. I have seen them.

The nursery keeps the ornamental and the useful separate. The list of Apples to be grown as decorative shrubs has now reached such a length that it daunts anyone trying to make a choice. Best perhaps to visit a small nursery where only a few of the best are offered than to risk your reason among the 40 or so that some of the big firms have for sale.

Here, for your delight, are a few that are really good, and even here unless you have broad acres you will, like a child in a sweet shop, find it hard enough to make up your mind.

Malus eleyi. It is rather large, but most Crabs can be kept tidy for many years as long as young shoots are cut back hard each summer. The flowers are a good red and the foliage also is red. The fruit is very like a deep red cherry.

M. aldenhamensis is similar but flowers later. It might be the better of the two for cold districts since frost can spoil Apple blossom and prevent it setting a crop.

M. purpurea. This is April-flowering and fruit and leaves are red. It is hardly worth planting this *and* either of the above, but it has pendant branches so is considered as a weeping form.

M. lemoinei is similar to *M. purpurea* but stiffer in habit.

M. floribunda is a very striking species with lovely pink flowers. If some shoots are cut in March they will flower in the house. The fruit is yellow.

M. hillieri has semi-double flowers which are red in bud but open to pink.

M. sargentii is slow-growing so especially good for the small garden. It has pure white flowers borne so thickly as to cover the whole tree. The Crabs are red.

Most of the Crabs are valued for their ornamental fruit, a few mainly for it. The best of them, some think, is John Downie which has small conical fruit orange-scarlet in colour.

Dartmouth Crab has rather larger red fruit which is covered with a bluish 'bloom'.

Cheal's Crimson is another good white-flowered variety.

And so I could go on. Our roadman says his granfer died of thirst because he could not decide which to drink first of the sixteen different beers he was offered. Well, it's like that with the ornamental Apples, so you venture into the nursery at your own peril.

And by the way if you live where wild Crabs grow in every hedgerow you will see some not at all inferior to the ones for which you will pay good money. They are usually too big for gardens, but there is nothing to stop anyone sowing seed for himself. Seedlings can be kept a reasonable size. The seed germinates very readily. Seedling Apples from eating Apples, or cooking ones, make wonderful small flowering trees, and you *might* raise an Apple worth eating, though, admittedly, that is unlikely. I have a seedling I found under my James Grieve and it is a very pretty Apple, a rich deep yellow. It is not bad eating either, a bit dry but *very* sugary and the flesh is soft and easy to chew.

'What a quarter have Authors made with Roses', said Culpeper, 'What a Racket they have kept.' Indeed he spoke truth, and he did not do so badly himself, giving them almost four whole pages in his *English Physitian*.

And what a racket they have kept with Apples. Almost as much as with Roses; it could well have been more. In legend and folklore and mythology Apples have figured prominently for thousands of years. They have been food and drink and medicine. They have been a comfort, 'Stay me with flagons, comfort me with apples'; a pungent country saying is 'as sure as God made little Apples. They turned the course of history when Discord threw in the Golden Apple to be presented to the most beautiful of the goddesses. Paris gave it to Venus and started the trouble that ended in the Greek-Trojan War and the fall and destruction of Troy.

It was because she paused to pick up the Golden Apples that Atlanta lost the race to Milanion and became his wife; the three sisters Hesperides guarded the Golden Apples which Hercules took, after killing a dragon, as the last of his twelve labours.

Newton's Apples helped him formulate the law of gravity – though that had been there all the time; William Tell gave us a good story, though rather weak history they say, by shooting an Apple off his son's head.

There is the Apple in the Arabian Nights that was a cure for all ills, while the Apples of Istakhar were sweet on one side, bitter on the other. By tasting the Apples kept by Idhunn, wife of Bragi, the gods of the Scandinavians preserved their youth. Sir John Mandeville said the Pygmies fed on the scent only of the Apples of Pyban. The Apples of Sodom were lovely to the eye, but ashes within, a myth that surely is also a parable.

The Apple of the eyes is a much-loved child; Apple-jack is an Apple turnover in East Anglia; in America it is a potent drink. An Apple-john was a variety that lasted two years. It matured by St John's Day, December 27, hence the name. 'I am withered like an old apple-john', Apple-pie bed is disorder: Apple-pie order is the opposite. An Apple a day keeps the doctor away. That could be so; a doctor told me something in the Apple – I can't remember what – destroys harmful bacteria. A mixture of Apple cider vinegar and honey taken regularly cures arthritis – or so they say.

'Kent, sir,' said Mr Jingle, 'everybody knows Kent – apples, cherries, hops and women.' On the other side of the country the juice of the Apple gives us one of the six Ws of Herefordshire: Wool, wood, water, wheat, women and wine.

And so one could go on; it gets tedious. But in conclusion I cannot refrain from offering you in its simplest form an easy recipe of my own.

Gather up your windfall apples or surplus ones; crush them or mince them. Put this revolting mess into a large tub or other container (not metal). To every six pounds of mash add three pounds of sugar. Put in boiling water to dissolve the sugar, using one gallon of water to six pounds of Apples. Allow to cool. While still warm add a teaspoonful of granulated yeast to the gallon.

This will ferment. Leave it alone until the mash sinks and the liquid clears. Bottle it.

My Apple wine will settle down as clear as a sunset sky on a frosty day. It has the colour of gold and a thin winey flavour all its own and it is deceptively easy to drink.

But it is a *very* potent brew. You have been warned!

If you use honey instead of sugar you get a sort of Mead – and after drinking that you understand how the Vikings, who drank lashings of it, were able to conquer half Europe, from the Orkneys to the Mediterranean.

OLEARIA   *Olearia haastii* is the New Zealand Daisy Bush. It is not usually accounted a choice shrub, the flowers being a rather dingy white, but on the other hand it is easy to grow, hardy, which other members of the family are not, evergreen, and does equally well in the air of towns and at the seaside. It is useful as a hedge, good as a windbreak. So it has its virtues, though it is perhaps better looking when not in flower. It grows easily from October cuttings so gives an inexpensive hedge or screen.

There are other species. *O. gunniana* has varieties with blue or mauve flowers but it is tender in most districts. *O. macrodonta* is fairly hardy in seaside districts but if not pruned will grow tall and leggy. Of the other score or so species available *O. semi-dentata* is more attractive than most of the family but yet more tender. If you have some really sandy stuff instead of soil, the sort Dean Hole said could be ploughed by a Dorking cock and a carving knife, try *O. traversii*. I've been told that in Cornwall it actually is used as a windbreak on practically pure sand.

PAEONIA   There are few gardeners who will not know the herbaceous tuberous-rooted Paeony, once a familiar sight in cottage gardens in early summer. The Tree Paeonies are shrubby species, equally handsome and colourful, but neither equally hardy nor equally easy to grow. They are slightly tender, or rather, as with Hydrangeas, the flower buds are. This weakness can be countered by planting in a warm, sheltered spot out of the early morning Sun (which would thaw out the frozen buds too quickly). In my experience the Tree Paeony is temperamental and the reason is not always easy to discover. Like the girl with the curl in the middle of her forehead, when it is good it is very very good, but when it is bad it is horrid. I have no Tree Paeonies myself but some of my friends have. In some gardens they flower wonderfully, while in others they sulk. Of course there must be a reason: soil or draughts or cold winds and if there is a cause there is a cure. But I do not know it; the obvious course is to give them the best possible conditions in every way. That is treatment few plants do not respond to.

Paeonia delavayi is from China. It will grow to some 5 feet. The flowers are crimson with yellow anthers and the seed cases are quite attractive.

P. lemoinei is not a true species but a hybrid and the flowers are yellow or yellow with some red shading.

P. lutea makes a pretty 3-foot shrub and also has yellow flowers, rather like a giant Buttercup.

P. suffruticosa is the most widely grown. The flowers are white and a number of pink to red shades. Most shrub nurseries have a number of varieties.

Paeonies are natives of China and Japan where they have always been highly regarded. They figure prominently in Chinese art and their history as cultivated plants goes back to the fifth century. The Paeony was known, or known of, in the west because 'a vary ancient Physition named Paeon, after whom it takes it name, used it to cure Pluto of a wound given him by Hercules.' In England it seems to have arrived a little before 1800 though it did not become common for the better part of another century. Indeed, there was good reason, for when it was available it was expensive and it always had the reputation of being

An unnamed Azalea hybrid makes a brilliant splash of colour in lime-free soil

Forsythia is excellent for flowering indoors in early spring

Viburnum fragrans (below) flowers outdoors all through the winter. The scent is equally welcome in the house

difficult. 'Just around the corner from Tree Paeonies stands the
Poor House' said one gardening writer.

A discouraging thought. Though they are still quite dear it is
not today as bad as that.

PHILADELPHUS This is the Mock Orange, known and loved both
for its fragrance and its beauty for some 400 years. For most of
that time it has been commonly and wrongly called Syringa.
Village gardeners always used that name, so before going further
we will get the matter put right, if you please.

Mock Orange is *Philadelphus*.

Lilac is *Syringa*.

The mistake arose because the first gardeners to grow them
thought they were in the same genus. They are not.

Gerard called the Mock Orange 'White Pipe'; Lilac he called
'Blew Pipe', but the dear man knew no better. I bet Mock
Orange will be called Syringa by village gardeners for a long time
to come. Why not? a Rose by any other name would smell as
sweet. But if you order Syringa you will get Lilac!

The Mock Orange is a beautiful flower, but in most gardens
is valued for its perfume. Not all growers have enjoyed it.
Gerard did not like it at all and having picked a bunch for a vase
found it so strong that he could not get to sleep. It was 'such a
ponticke and unacquainted savour, that they awaked me from
sleepe, so that I could not take any rest till I had cast them out
of my chamber.'

I have not heard of any medicinal use but the leaves will give
a cucumber sort of flavour to drinks and the flower petals have
been used to flavour tea. The flowers have been used in perfumery.

There are single and double varieties. *Philadelphus coronarius* is
the old single of cottage gardens and as far as I know is the most
strongly scented. I have a specimen, very tall but often cut back
hard to ground level, which I believe must be half a century old
at least and you can smell it yards away if you walk round the
garden on a warm summer evening. Sad to say it does not stay
long in bloom. Many of the modern double hybrids have little
scent. I had a magnificent bush of Virginal that literally was

E

completely covered with bunches of snowy, double flowers every year but I could get hardly a whiff of that penetrating fragrance, though some visitors said it *did* smell a little.

There are about 20 or so species and varieties. *P. coronarius* is still worth a place for its perfume and Virginal for the beauty of its double flowers. Another good double is Manteau d'Hermine, while Beauclerk and Belle Etoile are large-flowered singles. If you find the scent overpowering try Norma which has little of it.

A few of the family grow very tall, so if space is limited it is better to choose those that do not, though they respond to hard pruning, which should be done after flowering.

POLYGONUM One member of the Dock family is a climbing shrub, easy to grow almost anywhere. Its most notable feature is the rate it does grow. It will cover anything, shed, garage or what you like so rapidly, *and* then set out to conquer new territory that it needs to be cut down to size fairly regularly or it will bury the garden in greenery as effectively as whatever it was hid the Sleeping Beauty's palace. Perhaps that *was* what grew round it.

It has not really got a good common name. Some call it Russian Vine but that is not always recognised even by those who grow it. The correct title is *Polygonum baldschuanaicum*, which few can spell and fewer can pronounce. But all it means is that it came from Baldschuan in Bokhara. It grew at Kew from seed at the end of the nineteenth century. The flowers are tiny and white, borne in summer in such quantity that it could well be called foam-like. It may not be the most beautiful of shrubs but in suitable places it is a very useful one. There is a Japanese species, *P. multiflorum*, with pinkish flowers, less common, and I think less useful.

POTENTILLA This relation of the Strawberry is a true native of this country though a rare one. It has been grown in our gardens for hundreds of years, or it would be more correct to say that one species, *P. fruticosa*, has. Other species grow all across northern Europe and Asia and a lot of good forms have come from Tibet as well as other parts of the Himalayas. They are delightful shrubs with pretty yellow flowers rather like little single Roses, which is not surprising since they belong to the Rose family. Most nurseries will have up to a dozen or so species and varieties and though Farrar found them varying in height from 4 inches to 4 feet, on the average you can regard them as 3-foot shrubs. They have hybridised very freely so I think the botanists are a bit puzzled as to the names to use. But there is not a great deal of difference in them, except that the colour may be anything from white to deep yellow. *P. farreri* is good, so is Katherine Dykes; Abbotswood is about the best of the whites. There are, of course, many herbaceous species, some of them notable weeds; the five joined leaves and the flower petals have figured in heraldry. The herbalists had a long list of ailments in which it was effective, from 'Ifflation, Feaver and Pestilence' to 'Fals and bleeding'.

'This is an Herb of Jupiter and therefore strengthens the parts of the body that he rules.'

PRUNUS This is an enormous group of shrubs and trees, invaluable in the garden both for fruit and decoration. For the latter purpose the main divisions are

Almonds, *Prunus amygdalus;*
Apricots, *P. armeniaca;*
Bird Cherry, *P. padus;*
Cherry, *P. cerasus;*
Cherry Laurel, *P. laurocerasus;*
Portugal Laurel, *P. lusitanica;*
Purple Plum, *P. cerasifera* (or *P. pissardii*)

You might think these enough, but no indeed! If you want a sloe you find those under *P. spinosa;* the wild Plum, an edible but slightly bitter fruit often found growing in the hills, is *P. domestica,* while the Bullace is *P. insititia* ... and so on. The more you look the more you find. St Paul was warned 'much learning doth make thee mad' – the same might be said of trying to find your way through the species, sub-species and named garden varieties of the Prunus family.

Add to this that the botanists have played their usual games of musical chairs with many of the names – who turned my lovely red-leafed Purple Plum from *P. pissardii* into *P. cerasifera?* – and nobody could be blamed for becoming a little confused.

A look through a good catalogue shows about four pages of shrubs and trees of the genus. Say 25 to a page. That gives us a hundred. Now no gardener in his senses would want to plant a hundred ornamental Plums, Cherries and such. In fact, in a small garden one good flowering Cherry will be enough; some of the family can grow very large. The ones in the grounds of Tewkes-bury Abbey the last time I saw them were pretty hefty trees. So I must be very selective, giving only what I believe to be the best and the most suitable and if this would not be your choice, drop in at the nursery and I will agree that *your* choice is better than mine! I'm not, as we say up here, big-sorted!

But these would be *my* choice, for a garden such as my own.

ALMOND – You see these in warm districts in early spring, as early as March in some places. The bare boughs are crammed along their lengths with rich pink blossom. The common Almond is *P. amygdalus* (sometimes *P. communis*) but improved forms are *P. amygdalo-persica pollardii*, and another called Accolade. But now a warning. Almonds are hardy but they are from south Europe and in cold places they bud much too early to make much of a show in the cold spring winds. I have planted trees twice and the results have been very disappointing.

PEACH – *P. persica*. Clara Meyer is to my mind the best of the ornamental Peaches. It has double flowers a good strong pink in colour. But again it flowers, or tries to, much too early to do well in cold places. Against a sunny wall it may flower but it is a gamble and I do not know of a single specimen of this, or the fruiting varieties, in my own locality. The same applies to the Apricots, *P. armeniaca*. Peaches and Almonds are beautiful shrubs where they can be well-grown, but they should be sprayed when in the bud stage and again at leaf-fall as a protection against the distorted leaf blotches known as Peach leaf curl. Lime sulphur or Bordeaux Mixture are suitable, also there are proprietary sprays.

CHERRY – *P. padus* is our own wild Bird Cherry. Though it is a lovely little tree few gardeners would grow it except in a hedge or in woodland. The same may be said of *P. avium*, the Gean, the wild Cherry of the woods. Along the Marches in the Wye and Severn Valleys it whitens the landscape like snow every spring. It was as snow that A. E. Housman saw it: 'Loveliest of trees,' he called it.

> About the woodlands I will go
> To see the cherry hung with snow.'

Most gardeners, choosing ornamental Cherries, think first of the Japanese varieties. The naming and renaming of species (most of them are not true species) and the use of Japanese names for a host of them has resulted in a jolly good mix-up and tangle so that hardly anybody claims to know exactly which is which, and those who do claim to know generally do not.

Take one of the most popular, a variety people in thousands have planted with the name Hisakura on the label. Well, apparently it is not Hisakura, it is Kanzan. Or you may call it *P. serrulata sekiyama*, or *P. purpurascens*. Four men who had bought a tree under each of those four names – one apiece – could well have a mighty argument about which had the right one. Wigs on the green! It is quite dangerous to have all those names.

So I offer you five – five very good ones – but don't be surprised if they are called something else.

Kanzan – Strong erect tree. Large double, deep pink flowers in abundance.

Hisakura – Single rose pink flowers.

Tai-haku – Large single white flowers.

Shimidsu Sakura – This is pinkish in bud, pure white and double when open.

Kiku Shidare Zakura – Sometimes called Cheal's Weeping Cherry, which describes the habit. The flowers are pink and double.

For good measure I will add a great favourite of my own. *P. subhirtella autumnalis* is not one of the breathtakers. It is medium in size (I grow it as a standard) and comes into bloom any time from November to March depending on temperature and weather. The flowers are tiny, white or faintly pinkish and delicately scented. It is pretty when in flower. In my garden we seldom get the blossom until late March, but any time in mid-winter as soon as the tiny buds can be seen we pick branches, put them in water and in a warm room, or in a cold one, only more slowly, the flowers come out and shine like stars against the background of a dark wall or curtain.

A cheering sight, my masters!

CHERRY LAUREL – The common Laurel is *P. laurocerasus*. Left unpruned it will make a small tree 20 feet high and almost as much across. Used as screens they get sadly hacked in most gardens, but they are good sturdy things and they can, when carefully trimmed, make a stout hedge or a very fine windbreak. They are not showy either in flower or fruit, though individually the 'Cherries' are pretty – much the same to look at as a dark Cherry. There is a bit of a mystery about them: the fruits are said to contain prussic acid, which makes them a potent poison. Yet the leaves were used to give an almond flavour as early as the seventeenth century. Laurel water, a distillation from the leaves, was popular until two Irish women died through taking too much. Even then the use of the cordial went on. About 1780 there was a famous murder trial when a Captain Donaldson poisoned his brother-in-law with an extract of Laurel leaves. Donaldson was executed for the crime.

So it went on. Laurel water was undoubtedly poisonous to some degree, yet people continued to take it. It would seem that taken in moderation it was at least not a killer; if taken in excess the results could be fatal. The same can be said of other drugs, from alcohol to tobacco.

Philip Miller said the berries can be eaten 'in great Quantities without Prejudice', and Evelyn claimed that a 'not unpleasant' wine could be made from them.

Personally I would prefer a brew from a source a little less suspect.

Well, in all the best poison detective stories the victim always smelled faintly of Almonds. The conclusion seems to be that many of the family store up some quantity of hydrocyanic acid though as a rule it is so infinitesimally small as not to matter.

PORTUGAL LAUREL – *P. lusitanica*, is a handsome evergreen shrub that clips well, can be kept trimmed to any size, or used as a hedge though it will grow to the proportions of a small tree. The flowers come in long sprays in early summer. They are white but though they appear in good quantities are not very showy. But the cherry-like berries are pretty. They may be edible. I cannot find any mention of this anywhere and I have no intention of trying them. It is said that birds eat them: I have not seen them doing it, but the berries vanish from our bushes, so very likely they do. It is claimed that pheasants are very fond of them and the flesh of the birds that eat them is a particularly good flavour.

PLUM – There are a few good ornamental Plums for sale but though they are pretty enough I could never see much point in planting them. The eating Plums are such lovely things in flower and when bearing good crops of fruit that it has always seemed most sensible to plant a Victoria, or Greengage, or Coe's Golden Drop.

Mr Keble Martin calls the wild Plum, *P. domestica*. From this many of our eating Plums have evolved. I would not recommend *P. domestica* as a garden shrub: it would be very irritating to see a fine crop of fruit that looked tempting but was too bitter to be of use for anything.

The one shrub Plum that does need mention is the Purple Plum which you can still find listed as *P. pissardii*, as well as the more recent name of *P. cerasifera nigra*. What a lovely thing it is! Green is the colour for leaves every time but a few strong colours for contrast are almost essential. A Copper Beech would do but a full-grown Beech takes up too much room in a garden. So plant a Purple Plum. In early spring, very early in mild districts, the bare branches will be covered with small white or pale pink flowers and they are followed by the ruby-red leaves that are as rich in hue as light through a glass of Burgundy. A Purple Plum will grow tall and spread wide but it will stand hard cutting back and then will start all over again.

There is a purple-leafed Sloe and that too is worth a place. I would not plant a Blackthorn (Sloe). Not that it is not orna-mental; it is. But there are so many in the hedges and woods that we get our fill of them without giving up any of our precious space. Sloes with their lovely flowers are pretty and I'm told ripe Sloes make a fair wine. But they would have to be ripe. They give a pleasant flavour to gin; you just prick the fruit and soak in gin. An acquired taste, perhaps; gin isn't bad by itself!

The country folk call Blackthorn blossom time Blackthorn winter. I don't know if the cold weather brings out the flowers or if the snowy-white blossom everywhere brings the cold winds but sure enough the two seldom fail to appear at the same time.

Blackthorn spines are said to be poisonous and certainly enough hedgers and roadmen have had painful festering wounds on hands and fingers through these vicious little thorns. This happened so commonly that many a labourer carried a charm to protect him from blood-poisoning. As a rule the charms were written down and carried in a pocket.

Here is one from Cornwall – similar ones are found in many districts:

> Happy man that Christ was born,
> He was crowned with a Thorn;
> He was pierced through the skin,
> For to let the poison in:
> But His five wounds, so they say,
> Closed before He passed away;
> In with healing, out with Thorn;
> Happy man that Christ was born.

PYRACANTHA The best of this genus are known as Firethorns and while their little Hawthorn flowers are pleasant, it is for their plentiful berries that most of them are grown. They are used mostly as wall plants and are thickly covered with orange or red berries from early autumn onwards. There are no cultural difficulties though in cold areas they are not reliable croppers in the open, mainly because, like their cousins the Apples, late frosts and cold spring winds interfere with pollination. In height they may reach 15 feet or more. The most popular of the family is *Pyracantha coccinea lalandii*, which bears masses of orange-red berries.

The old demon of name changing creeps in again. *P. augustifolia* is also known as *Cotoneaster augustifolia*. It has distinctive narrow leaves which are felt-like underneath and the berries are orange.

There are other species, but those two are the best for most gardens. If you would like yellow berries for a change try *P. crenulata flava* (which to make things more amusing may be found as *P. rogersiana flava*!) and yellow ones you shall have.

The generic name comes from the Greek *pyr* (fire), *acanthus* (thorn) but the Blackbird cares not what the name may be; he loves it for its fruit alone and may, if allowed to, gobble up the lot in a very short time.

RHODODENDRON As mentioned earlier these and the Azaleas are botanically the same but most gardeners like to keep them separate, if only to simplify things when it comes to choosing which shall be planted. There are so many that I am sure it is wise to buy from a small (but *very* good) nursery. I have nothing but admiration for the specialists but their lists may contain a few hundred species and a few hundred more named varieties. Choosing the best is not easy, though of course they will always choose for you.

There is one important point about culture, generally well known. These shrubs will not grow or will not grow satisfactorily, where there is lime in the soil. Where the soil is suitable they grow so well and are so fine in bloom that everybody who sees them wants a few in his own garden. Well there are ways of growing them and if extra care and trouble are taken with them it is possible to have them, but there is an element of risk. In gardens as a general rule it is as well to accept the natural limitations Nature imposes on us. I do not try to grow tender shrubs on my cold hillside. The risk of disappointment and loss are too great and in any garden it is best to grow well that which *will* grow. This is a personal rule, but perhaps Rhododendrons should be allowed to be the proverbial exception.

If you want them but could not just put them in with any hope of success I know of two procedures and anyone can work out variations of those.

One is to excavate soil and fill the hole with a compost of peat, old manure, leafmould and sand. Peat would be the basis of this mixture; the leafmould and manure would supply plant food, the sand give drainage. Where very little lime is present a Rhododendron might thrive in that for a long time. But if there is much lime present either the roots will eventually reach it, or some may seep in in solution. And then you must start all over again.

A better method is to make a raised bed on concrete or slate slabs. It could be contained by a low wall, or better still by turfs of peat. These, by the way, in some of the more remote hamlets in my part of the country are still dug out of the bogs in the hills, dried and stacked for use as winter fuel. A few years ago many farms and cottages used nothing else on their fires, which were never allowed to go out. In those times it was a day's work for a man, horse and cart to fetch a load of coal. Nowadays a lorry would deliver a load, but peat is free while coal is not! Coal may be used a little more than it was fifty years ago, but the stacks of peat on the hills is still a familiar sight in summer.

I digress, but the point is that if you are near a supply, peat blocks could cost very little more than cost of transport; if you are not near a supply the blocks would have to be bought from a merchant who sells horticultural peat.

Whether you contained your bed inside a peat or stone wall the compost needed would be the same as the one already recommended. It is possible to grow some lime-hating plants in a raised bed of peat blocks alone, but I do not think this would contain enough nourishment for such hearty growers as Rhododendrons. Watering, with lime-free water, would need attention in some seasons.

The other possibility is to plant in the ordinary way and use a substance called Sequestrene, mentioned earlier, which counters the action of lime. The shrubs have to be watered with it. Some gardeners have had very good success with it but as I have a soil in which Rhododendrons grow and flourish, even seeding themselves sometimes, I have never had occasion to use it.

To choose a good selection of these incomparable shrubs is easy enough; to say you have chosen the very best is another matter. They come in all sizes, shapes and colours, and new garden hybrids arrive as regularly as the seasons.

Very roughly, there are two main classes. There are the species, which are the wild Rhododendrons that have been found in various parts of the world. Largely the plant hunters have brought the best, often as seeds, from eastern Asia, particularly from the lower slopes of the Himalayas.

Many of these have been cross-bred and have given us named garden forms, hybrids, often called cultivars. A lot are alike, both in form and in colour. In choosing you can hardly go wrong if all you want is a lusty shrub with flowers of a certain colour. The specialists have a lot to choose from: many smaller places keep only a few. From the former you can get almost anything you fancy: from the latter you have less choice, but an easier one.

Pink Pearl is said to be the most popular hybrid ever raised, so unless you want to be different, start with that. You may see it in lots of other gardens but it is none the worse for that. Cunningham's White is one of the best whites. For scarlet you could do worse than C. B. van Ness, while Blue Peter is lavender blue. Goldsworth Orange is more yellow than red: Diane is paler.

That covers some shade of each of the main colours available. Others are darker; some are lighter. Some flowers have spots on them; in others the spots have spread into blotches.

The choice of species is not so simple and is made more difficult because, while some are the true wild types others have been bred from these and there are the usual confusing synonyms in the names. Another point about species is that while some are real beauties, a few are more interesting to the specialist and collector than beautiful in the garden.

On the whole these worries are for the specialists and they know how to find their way about. A good book for those who would like guidance in the less-known paths is Frederick Street's *Hardy Rhododendrons*, a most readable book in spite of Mr Street being an expert. The index contains a long list of names, but nothing to what you can find in the Rhododendron Society's handbooks. Mr Street has also written a splendid book on Azaleas.

R. ponticum is the old-fashioned type, common, easy, and very beautiful in flower, though the purple shades lack the brilliance of modern hybrids. It is good anywhere, in sun or in shade, reliable and quick-growing. It makes a splendid hedge.

R. cinnabarinum is a lovely shrub with tubular red blooms.

R. discolour flowers in July. The flowers are white and very large. It is strong-growing, up to 20 feet, so needs cutting back occasionally, immediately after flowering.

R. yunnanense grows to about 8 feet with flowers of a silvery pink spotted with brown. Most Rhododendrons have to be layered but this species grows well from cuttings.

It has been mentioned that Rhododendrons come in all sizes. There are some that really are miniature and they are lovely in a rock garden. My own favourite, because it does so well for me, is *R. impeditum*. The whole bush is hardly more than 6 inches tall, though the couple I have are spreading widely. In spring the whole bushy mound is literally covered with purple-blue flowers. A hybrid of this is Blue Tit which is very similar but a good deal taller.

R. ferrugineum is sometimes called the Alpen Rose. You can see it growing thickly on the lower slopes of the Alps and the Pyrenees. It is bigger than *impeditum* and so are the flowers, which are rose-crimson. This little shrub blossoms in June.

The Rhododendron as a rule has been regarded in this country mainly for ornament. In the east the timber of some of the species has been used in many ways, not exactly commercially but by the inhabitants for their needs, from yak saddles to firewood. The leaves of *R. chrysanthum* were the chief ingredient in a medicine. It appears to have been a narcotic and sedative so could have deadened pain. But little seems to be known about it and from the little I know it appears the family is not one to trifle with. The Azalea honey that temporarily laid out Xenophon's men is paralleled by that made from some Rhododendrons, as it would they being the same plant botanically. Poisoning from honey gathered from the flowers has been reported from various parts of the world. But always there are what seem to be contradictory reports. In Tibet they made, very likely still do, a candied sweetmeat of the individual flowers. I have heard that the scent of some Alpine kinds can cause headache, and I have read somewhere, I have forgotten where, that explorers, warming themselves by Rhododendron-wood fires became ill after inhaling fumes from the smoke. Nobody, as far as I can find out, has isolated the drug that must be in the plant somewhere, but neither candied Rhododendron flowers nor Rhododendron log fires come much within my experience.

RHUS This is the Sumach and it is another genus to be handled with care. Two species should never be planted in gardens (they have been) and luckily nowadays they are never to be found in any catalogue though when they were first introduced many people did grow them and some of the early gardening books did not mention how dangerous they were. It appears that, as with the greenhouse Primulas, some people are very sensitive to them while others can handle them and come to no harm. In America, where they came from, the risks were well known to the Red Indians and then to the settlers, for the common names are Poison Ivy and Poison Oak and as early as 1668 one of them was called Poyson-weed. That great shrub authority W. J. Bean gives an account of a gardener who had to spend months in hospital after propagating Poison Ivy from cuttings. The dangerous property is in a substance called toxicodendrol which is found in the sap. This has a corrosive effect on skin, on some skins more than others, and not being soluble in water it is difficult to wash it off.

The two species are *Rhus toxicodendron* and *R. radicans*.

Four other species are held to be harmless and are grown in gardens. But I think the sap of any of them is suspect and I am not alone in holding this view. I would advise any gardeners with delicate skins, certainly those who get Primula rash, to manage without the Sumachs.

But they are handsome shrubs and they do give magnificent leaf colour in autumn.

The four permissible species are *R. cotinus*, *R. cotinoides*, *R. typhina* and *R. glabra*.

R. cotinus is called the Smoke Bush because the flower pannicles are so finely divided that they give a smoke-like appearance to the bush.

R. cotinoides is similar but has larger leaves. It is regarded as the best of the genus for autumn colour.

R. typhina. This is the Stag's Horn Sumach, so named on account of the pyramidal inflorescence. It also has very large pinnate leaves.

R. glabra has smooth stems, very hairy in some forms, and the typical pinnate leaves.

RIBES   Flowering Currant. How pleasant to turn to something that can be recommended without reservation. It might be called a cottage garden shrub. At least it grew in almost every small garden where I was brought up and was planted so widely that it seemed to be typically native. That would be an error, for it came from America and cannot have been in poor men's gardens very long, for it was only introduced in 1825. It would have had a spell in botanical gardens, then in those of the well-to-do before the nurseryman and the ordinary gardener got hold of it.

Once started the spread could have been rapid since it grows very easily from cuttings and also from seeds.

Two of some dozen species are good garden shrubs. *Ribes*

sanguineum is the best known but is not as highly regarded as it ought to be and even where it is grown it is relegated to some out-of-the-way corner where often it is not seen to advantage. Grown well, provided a real *sanguineum* (blood-red) shade is grown, it can be spectacular. It is one of the earliest spring shrubs and the scarlet pendant groups of flowers shine out on a dull March or April day like a good deed in a naughty world. Though it is hardy I have known the flowers to brown a little after a really vicious frost so it deserves a warm sheltered spot so that it can cheer us while winter seems to be still lingering on the doorstep.

The best coloured form is *R. sanguineum atrorubens*. It should be pruned fairly hard after flowering so that it can make plenty of good strong young wood that will bear the next year's flowers.

R. aureum is the Golden Currant, less showy than the red kind, but well worth a place, because the flowers have a delicious scent. There may be large black berries but only, I think, where spring is fairly mild.

Of the others available *R. americanum* is good for autumn leaf colour and *R. speciosum* has flowers something like small Fuchsias. *R. gayanum*, with yellow flowers, is evergreen.

There are species native to Europe and Asia and from them the Red Currant and the Gooseberry are descended.

ROBINIA These are often called Acacias but the true Acacia is the Mimosa and species of that are tender or at the best susceptible to frost damage. Most Robinias are trees and much too large for gardens, unless grown as a single specimen, say in a large lawn. Two, *Robinia hispida* and *R. kelseyi* grow only to shrub size or can be kept so and fortunately are among the most attractive in form and in flower.

R. hispida is known as the Pea Acacia. It grows some 6 feet tall. The flowers are in clusters of pea-shaped blossoms. They come out in June but often persist all through summer. The colour is a rich rose-pink. *R. kelseyi* is very similar but perhaps a little taller. Some say it is the better of the two but there is not much in it. The only thing is, the branches of *R. kelseyi* are brittle and easily damaged by high winds so the shrub needs a sheltered position. Sometimes there are attractive seed-pods in autumn.

The Robinia was introduced from America about 1740 but commemorates a much earlier gardener, Jean Robin, who about the end of the sixteenth century was gardener to Henri IV of France at the Louvre. This good man deserved the honour of being remembered in the name of a lovely shrub, for he grew, so we are told, more than a thousand different plants and corresponded with two of our own most-famous gardeners, John Gerard and John Parkinson. The latter had one of the tree Acacias in his collection.

ROMNEYA   Romneya is the Tree Poppy. This Californian plant is a most beautiful thing. It has large satin-white flowers which hardly need description since they really do resemble poppies. The shrub has a reputation for being tender but most authorities agree it will still flower in most gardens without protection. I think it does do best in warmth – what Californian would not – but any good soil suits it. The plants are best pruned to the ground in spring and the blooms come on new shoots over quite a long season, June to October in a genial climate. The height is some 4 feet or more. Commercial propagation is by root cuttings but for getting the odd extra plant you can detach a single rooted stem and grow it on separately. Young plants taken in this way are best started in a frame or a cold house.

Romneya coulteri is the species usually planted. There are two others, *R. trichocalyx* and *R. hybrida* but they are so like *R. coulteri* that there seems no point in planting them. The shrub is named in honour of Dr Romney Robinson a nineteenth-century astronomer who had been named after Romney the artist. Robinson's father had been a pupil of Romney.

ROSA   Sweeping statements just howl out for contradiction, but it is safe to say that the Shrub Roses are not very well known, certainly not nearly as well known as they deserve to be and therefore are not as widely planted as they ought to be. It is also fairly safe to say that if gardeners *did* plant them they would be very well pleased with the results of their labours – and very likely surprised by them.

For a hundred people who go to a nursery in search of Roses, not one is likely to be looking for a Shrub Rose. With container planting gaining popularity, which means growers looking round more critically, the position may change a little. More than once I have asked for a Shrub Rose, to find them sold out to gardeners who have come, seen and conquered.

The Rose position briefly is this. For centuries, actually for thousands of years, men have been growing Roses. They started with the wild ones; these were crossed with other wild ones, or got on with the job themselves – a promiscuous lot the Roses – and variations and hybrids and so on crept in. Time went by and the Roses grown were, on the whole, vigorous bushes bearing large crops of scented, often rather formless blooms. Many bore only one crop in the summer, but a few were in flower, more or less, over many months.

Within the last few centuries gardeners began more and more to take a hand in breeding new flowers. This eventually resulted in the hybrid teas and they have now been the most popular garden roses for nearly a century. They, like good wine, need no praise. In form, colour, sometimes perfume they are to most gardeners the most beautiful flowers in the world.

Like other Beauty Queens they have qualities that make them less than perfect. They do not make good shrubs; as plants they often lack form; they sometimes need cosseting; they are greedy (flowers); they suffer easily from pests and diseases . . . Have they other weaknesses? Possibly, but those will do.

Not for one single moment am I suggesting that we should do without them. But hybrid teas are not for the shrub garden. Beauty Queens are breath-taking; healthy, vigorous, not-so-glamorous Dairymaids (are there any these days?) are often more useful.

When the teas arrived the majority of the Shrub Roses were forgotten and there was a time when a lot went out of cultivation. But discerning Rose growers continued to appreciate them. They collected them, grew them, cultivated them, occasionally gave away (or sold) a few of them. Many good ones really *were* lost, but it is surprising how many survived. Nowadays I do not think there is a nursery in the country that has not at least a few of the best to sell.

Their faults are few; their virtues many. Some are a poor shape in bloom compared with the teas. Some are rather odd in colour, often what you might call cold-hand purple. Some have a short flowering season, though that is a fault in many other shrubs.

But they grow to full size rapidly; they will grow well on poor soil (though there is no need to starve them!). They are rarely ruined by pests and are very resistant to disease – I have never sprayed one for anything – they need little pruning beyond tidying up and removing old, dead or weak shoots. Many bear crops of lovely hips. Most, large or small, have a good bush form and most when well spread out cover their allotted space so thoroughly that they are grand labour-savers.

If I say any more I shall sicken you with over-praise. So we will leave it there.

By Rose species we mean wild Roses of this and other lands. But hybridising has gone on so much, both artificial and natural, that it is doubtful if some of the so-called species *are* true species. The Shrub Roses are generally found under three names: Rose species and their named varieties; Bush Roses, also under garden names, and Old Fashioned Roses.

These are often divided into classes and I think if we keep these to twelve we shall get in most of the best. But to select and recommend can easily lead to the rapping of knuckles!

Anyhow, here are my twelve groups:

Rosa alba – An old Rose that has been grown in our country for centuries. It makes a large bush; the blooms which come out in July are pale colour and strongly scented.

Bourbon Roses – A cross between China and Damask Roses. Very free-growing, though not very bushy (in my garden). Marvellous fragrance and good colour and nearly always in flower if grown on a wall. I like most, Zéphirine Drouhin, and Souvenir de la Malmaison.

Rosa centifolia – This is the Cabbage Rose, lovely and fragrant. It is old but not, say the scientists, as ancient as has been believed. My own bushes, taken many years ago from a ruined cottage in Pembrokeshire, have rich pink blooms but there are varieties in other colours.

Moss Rose – This is a sport (variation) from the Cabbage Rose, with thorns that have decided to be non-thorns. These make up the hair-like 'moss'. Blanche Moreau is a good variety.

R. damascena is the Rose of Damascus, or the Damask Rose. It was possibly, or even probably, introduced by the Crusaders. A romantic flower this, the Rose of the poets and troubadours, the flower of Attar of Roses. A very nice Damask is Rose de Quatre Saisons. I doubt if it does flower in the four seasons but it does its best and is usually quite good in autumn.

R. gallica, the French Rose, is said to have been used in medicines in Persia earlier than 1,000 BC. It was grown extensively at Provins near Paris for medical purposes, which gives it the other name of Provins Rose (*not* Provence Rose, that is another kind).

The Austrian Briars are not as striking as some but have become important in breeding as they have helped in giving strong, dark-green foliage and some of the most striking colours in flowers. Persian Yellow is a good choice to plant.

R. moschata – The Musk Rose of Shakespeare – and other poets. Musks have a delicious scent. The pink Felecia is a good one to plant, but almost any you find in a nursery would be as good.

Noisette Rose – A hybrid between the Musk and the China Roses, but probably there are others mixed up in their ancestry. The lovely Gloire de Dijon is sometimes found in lists as a Noisette, but it is probably mostly Tea. The best of this group is Maréchal Niel, very beautiful, very scented, but, alas, sometimes temperamental! Another good one you can get easily is William Allen Richardson.

R. rubriginosa – Sweet Briar. This should need no praise. It would pass for *R. canina*, the Dog Rose, were it not for the fragrance of its leaves and young stems. Sweet Briar makes a good informal hedge.

R. rugosa – A Rose from China that has often been used for budding. It is not a good stock as it suckers too freely. But a small thicket of one of the named varieties, say *R. rugosa rubra*, is a lovely sight when it is in full bloom.

R. spinosissima is the very spiny Scots Briar. It thrives in poor soil and grows into a rounded thicket which will usually smother out weeds. A lovely named variety is Stanwell Perpetual with pink buds and pink-white flowers.

Some growers are now introducing hybrids which they list as Modern Shrub Roses. These have, or should have, all the good points of the older flowers and some that belong to the newest types. Some very promising shrubs have appeared and, with the least encouragement from gardeners, more and even better ones should come. So it is almost a duty as well as a pleasure to plant at least one Modern Shrub Rose among your shrubs. If you do not know them you could do worse than order Constance Spry.

Among wild Roses I have four favourites. They are *R. cantabrigensis*, which might be a hybrid, *R. hugonis*, *R. moyesii*, the brick-red Chinese species, and *R. xanthina*, which is yellow.

ROSMARINUS   Rosemary. This has nothing to do with Rose or Mary, but is the dew (*ros*) of the sea, a reminder that it thrives in coastal districts. It seems to be able to tolerate lots of wind and lots of the horrid corrosive salt that comes on those winds. But it will grow happily anywhere and is good on chalk. It is an upright little shrub though in my garden it has a tendency to sprawl and, again in my specimens, the base of the little trunk twists and looks sinewy, not unattractively, like the bole of an ancient tree. The leaves are very aromatic and so are the pale blue flowers which come out in June. It is a plant of the Mediterranean countries so appreciates plenty of sun though it is perfectly hardy. Like its relative, the Lavender, it will make an attractive low hedge and an inexpensive one too, since it grows readily from cuttings.

Some half-dozen species and varieties are offered by the larger nurseries but the commonest, *R. officinalis*, is, I think, the best. *R. pyramidalis* is said to be better for low hedges. There is a prostrate form that was *R. prostratus* when I first grew it but is now *R. humilis*. This is useful for the rock garden or for a dry wall.

Rosemary is one of our oldest shrubs. It is thought it may have been introduced in Roman times. In the library of Trinity College, Cambridge, there is a manuscript written by 'a clerk of the school of Salerno' copied by 'danyel bain' dealing with the virtues of this most respected of shrubs.

'It uniteth the boones and causeth goode and gladdeth and lighteth alle men that use it. The leves layde under the heade whanne a man slepes, it doth away evell spirites and suffereth not to dreeme fowle dremes ne to be afeade. But he must be out of deedely synne.'

How people loved Rosemary all down the centuries! What was its magic? The herb of remembrance, a disinfectant for sick-rooms, a flavouring, a medicine. There is so much literature about it that it needs a chapter to do it full justice. The flowers were originally white but on the Flight into Egypt the Virgin Mary spread her cloak over a bush and they turned blue in her honour. It continues to grow for 30 (33?) years, the age of Jesus when he died, and then grows no taller.

'As for Rosemary,' said Thomas More, 'I lette it runne all over my garden walls, not onlie because my bees love it, but because it is the herb sacred to remembrance and to friendship, whence a sprig of it hath a dumb language.'

RUBUS The Bramble you might think could well be left out. Most of us have more trouble getting rid of it than introducing it. But not all the family is as rough as the respected (when in hedges) wild Blackberry.

A strange tribe it is too, gipsyish, wild, but having its virtues when you come to know it better. It is related to the Rose, but with three or four times the species and even more hopelessly mixed as to names.

Yet there are many that are ornamental and there might be

room for one or two of these in a barren corner where nothing else will grow. The berries hardly need mention and some of the cultivated kind like the Himalayan Blackberry are enormous and have a fine flavour. On the other hand the flavour of the most ornamental members of this genus is as tasteless as Dead Sea fruit.

Rubus amabilis is a Chinese species that is not too invasive. The stems are an attractive purple colour, the flowers large, for a Blackberry, and the fruits red and edible.

R. fraseri has large rose-coloured flowers and could be useful because it will grow under trees.

R. odoratus is another good Bramble for use as ground cover under trees.

R. spectabilis also might be used as ground cover in shade. The flowers are magenta and the stems grow erect up to 6 feet in height.

R. thyrsoides flore-pleno has double white flowers; another, *R. leucarpushas*, white flowers. I cannot find a nursery that stocks this. Nor do I know who sells *R. phoenicolasius* though I have seen it growing. It is a pretty thing with red bristles growing so thickly that the stems seem to be covered with red fur.

One could hardly claim that the Brambles are choice shrubs but in gardens with difficult corners a few of the prettiest could be very useful.

According to Culpeper the astringent qualities of the Bramble, fruit, leaves or stems, made it valuable in treating wounds or sores and such troubles as ulcers in the mouth. Or you could dye your hair with it. 'The leavs boyled in Ly and the Head washed therewith, healeth the Itch and the running sores thereof, and maketh the Hair black.'

Ruta is Rue, a herb that has been known and valued for centuries. It contains a drug called rutin which is, or was during the war, used in the treatment of high blood pressure. In commerce rutin is generally made from Buckwheat, an American plant. Rue is a rather slow-growing shrub and it would take a long time to collect any quantity of the drug from it.

As long ago as the time of the Greek Empire it was valued for its medicinal uses. The old English name, Herb of Grace, was on account of those qualities.

Shakespeare knew it: 'Here in this place I'll set a bank of Rue, sour herb of grace.' Culpeper has nearly two pages of uses for it from 'Poysons and Plague' to 'Belly Obstructions'. Milton recorded that 'Euphrasy and Rue' were used by an angel to restore Adam's sight.

Apart from the use in high blood pressure, which for all I know may have been superseded by a new synthetic drug, it is still used in some nervous diseases. It is too bitter to be much good in cookery but the leaves, I am told, will keep away fleas (we hardly see them nowadays) and probably moths. It was much used in the law courts in olden days as a disinfectant when gaols smelled more foul than we expect them to today.

There is only one species I know, *Ruta graveolens*. It grows about 3 feet tall and about as much across. The leaves are an attractive bluish-green and the flowers yellow. A few bushes make attractive ground cover, either in the open or under taller shrubs. A little hedge of it could be very attractive. The scent of the leaves is pleasant rather than delicious, though some people find it objectionable.

SALIX It is not out of place to include the Willow because the flowers (catkins) of some species, the Pussy Willows, are a delightful sight in early spring when so little else is in bloom.

But size will keep most of the Willows out of most of our gardens, though it is possible to plant a small standard Willow and keep it to reasonable dimensions by pollarding it, as described earlier in the book under 'Pruning'. If you feel that pollarding (an ancient practice, by the way) is mutilation then few Willows are for you. By the banks of the Thames, and other rivers, a healthy tree will go up to 60 feet or more.

Out of a score or so species *Salix gracilistyla* can be recommended as it grows to about 6 feet. The catkins are attractive and so are the leaves. *S. repens* makes a shapely spreading bush with yellow catkins.

S. babylonica, which has other specific names, the most suitable of which is *tristis* or sad, is the Weeping Willow of Babylon beside which the exiled Israelites sat down and wept. Not that they wept for long: indeed, for those times and considering they were captured in war, Babylon treated them not at all unkindly. SAMBUCUS   The Elder is hardly a garden shrub though it is one that on poor soils and in difficult districts will give a good account of itself. In the hedgerows and woods it is almost the first of the white flowers after the snow of the Wild Cherry has gone. Inside the garden, say the grumblers, we have too much yellow. It has just occurred to me that white is almost as persistent outside: Cherry, Blackthorn, May, often the Apple blossom, though that is pink sometimes. Then come the flat heads of the Wayfaring Tree, that poor relation of the Snowball Tree, and now Elder flowers everywhere. There may be a reason for this continuous show of bridal purity on the part of Nature; I've not worked it out.

Apart from difficult gardens, plagued by industrial smoke or heavily shaded by trees the only Elder I can recommend without reservation, provided you like coloured leaves, is *Sambucus nigra aurea*. Sometimes called Golden Elder its leaves are as bright as the proverbial, but never seen, guinea, and it shines from afar as brightly as Forsythia.

For those who do appreciate this shrub, common or no, there are *S. fructeo luteo* with yellow berries and *S. nigra flore pleno* with double flowers.

Outside the garden it is a different story; the humble shrub, despised by most gardeners, suddenly turns from Frog to Fairy Prince. It is one of the most-renowned trees in the country. There is enough literature about it in the Herbals to fill a sizeable book. John Evelyn in *Sylva* says the wood is useful for cogs of mills, butchers skewers 'and such tough employments'. About its virtues as medicine he grows almost lyrical. 'If the medical properties of the leaves, bark, berries &c. were thoroughly known, I cannot tell what our countryman could ail, for which he might not fetch a remedy from every hedge, either for sickness or wound: The inner bark of Elder, applied to a burning takes out the fire immediately; that, or in season the buds, boiled in water-grewel for a breakfast has effected wonders in a fever; and the decoction is admirable to assuage inflammations and tretrous humours, and especially the scorbut . . . ' and so on. It makes you smile. Or it would if you did not remember all the silly brews, pills, lotions, gargles, cosmetics and what not on which we spend millions of pounds. We haven't really changed much. Fools and their money are soon parted. Some of the modern drugs do work: so did some of the Old Wives Remedies.

Mind, Evelyn did not praise without warning. The smell was dangerous. 'A certain house in Spain, seated amongst many Elder trees, diseased and killed almost all the inhabitants, which when at last they were grubbed up, became a very wholesome and healthy place.

The herbalist Culpeper, strangely, did not list the Elder's uses, saying Dwarf Elder, a herbaceous plant, was more potent. He appeared to think they were related, but he was better as a doctor (we hope!) than as a botanist. Dwarf Elder is the Gout-weed, that terrible thing to keep us from too much pride. It is a member of the *Umbelliferae* family, while the Elder belongs to one called *Caprifoliaceae*, to which unfamiliar tribe belong the Viburnums and Honeysuckle.

In *Flowers and Flower Lore* (1883) Hilderic Friend has indexed twenty references to Elder. It would be tedious to mention them all. The flowers gave Gerard inspiration for one of his happiest phrases: 'The floures grow on spoky rundles.' I don't think those are in any dictionary I possess. He mentions a bit of country lore – 'it is planted about Cony-boroughs for the shadow of the Conies.'

Judas hanged himself on an Elder: we are told so in *Piers Plowman*:

> Judas he japed
> With Jewen silver,
> And sithen on an eller
> Hanged himself.

Sir John Mandeville saw the actual tree!

The shrub as well as a medicine had all manner of magical properties. The leaves, hung outside a door, kept away witches; not fairies, though, for a baby in a cradle of Elder wood might be well pinched by those wee folk.

But whatever you care to believe, of the folklore there is no doubt at all. Excellent wine can be made of both the flowers and the fruit. The latter was once used to adulterate port. More recently I have tasted port that could be improved by it! *Good* Elderberry wine is not to be despised.

SANTOLINA   This is called Lavender Cotton, a charming dwarf shrub with grey leaves and yellow flowers that has nothing to do with either Lavender or Cotton. I don't think one would grow it for its flowers, but the foliage is pretty and strongly aromatic. It can be used as ground cover, as edgings to borders and paths or as a low hedge. It will grow almost anywhere but is best suited on places like hot sunny banks. Being a plant of Mediterranean hillsides it loves dry sunbaked spots. It grows very freely from cuttings at almost any time of the year. The aroma is too strong for use as a food flavouring, but it is said to be excellent when dry as a moth and insect repellent. When women made their own 'simples' that was its chief use. A vermifuge (worm expelling) medicine for children was made from it in olden days.

Santolina incana, more often listed now as *S. chamaecyparissus* – which is not as easy to spell or pronounce, is the species chiefly listed, but there is a form *name* which is more dwarf. *S. neapolitana* is supposed to be a little taller, while *S. virens* has green foliage.

SENECIO   This is an evergreen with handsome silvery leaves and yellow daisy-like flowers in summer. It has the reputation of being on the tender side but it thrives in my garden which (you may have already gathered!) does not enjoy a Riviera type of climate in winter. Occasionally a particularly hard spell treats it a bit roughly but so far the bushes have never failed to recover. In any case it is very easy to replace losses from cuttings. *Senecio greyii*, the most common species, can reach 4 feet though the average so far as I have seen is well under this. The whole shrub, with me, tends to sprawl, which suits me very well since a few plants at the top of a warm bank pour down it and soon makes excellent ground cover.

Senecio is a good seaside shrub and there you can see some really fine specimens. In full bloom they are a really cheerful sight. They appear to thrive on salt winds and thin sandy soils.

If you grow *S. greyii* (have seen this spelled *greyi*) do not add *S. laxifolius;* it is either the same or practically so. *S. monroi* has wavy leaves, may be tender, but is grand near the sea. *S. rotundi-folia* has round tough leaves that will stand any gale that ever blew.

SORBUS This genus contains mainly trees, such as the lovely Whitebeam. Most of them are not for gardens. The one exception is *Sorbus aucuparia*, the Mountain Ash or Rowan. This is a British native and seems to grow all over the country. When it does grow on mountains it is usually stunted and dwarf in stature, but in the lowlands and fertile ground it can reach near forest tree size. The most satisfactory way to grow it in the garden is to pollard it, and let it form a head of branches. I know some gardeners do not like this lopping of branches, claiming it to be unnatural and ugly. But much we do in gardens is unnatural and as for ugliness that, like beauty, often lies in the eye of the beholder. My best Rowan is very near the house and unchecked cuts out too much light. It is then due for treatment. But that only happens once in many years. In between it looks handsome and many birds sing in the branches thereof. The flowers are creamy white and strongly scented. They are followed by beautiful scarlet berries and the leaves colour well in autumn.

There are other species of the Mountain Ash. *S. gracilis*, which is rather rare, is a Japanese kind; *S. hupehensis* comes from China as do many of the less familiar ones such as *S. pluripinnata* which has many leaflets making up its pinnate leaves. But on the whole the differences are not great and the foreign species are not more handsome than those you can transplant from any mountain woodland or hedgerow.

The shiny red berries provide one of the minor personal mysteries of my own garden. When the berries turn red, thrushes,

I think it is mainly thrushes but there may be others, come and eat the lot – every one. Almost before they are ripe a sudden attack is made and however much I make shooing noises, in a matter of a day or two the whole crop is gone. Yet the same day I can go to the woods and the hedgerows within a mile and the berries, untouched, are as scarlet as a guardsman's tunic, and as ripe as a Blenheim apple at Easter.

Why *my* berries? It is very odd! The only explanation would appear to be that the birds like company. This does not happen occasionally. It has happened every year, so far as I can remember, since we came to this house over twenty years ago. When you come to think of it there must have been quite a few generations of birds in that time.

All along the Welsh-English border the Mountain Ash is called Witty, and that is a corruption of Witchen (tree) because it is 'a preservative against fascinations and evil spirits.'

Evelyn called it Quick-beam. He advised or noted the use of the timber for husbandman's tools, goads, wheelwright's use and planks: 'our fletchers commend it for bows next to Yew.' Apparently a statute of Henry VIII mentions it for that purpose.

'It is excellent fuel,' he says. Not along the Marches, I may add, where I do not think any countryman would be so brave as to make a fire of Witty, even on the coldest day. I used to burn it, but I was warned it was terribly unlucky so I haven't burned any since! As the old woman said when reproved for curtsying whenever the Devil's name was mentioned: 'No harm being on the safe side!'

'Some highly commend the juice of the berries, which, fermenting of itself, if well preserved, makes an excellent drink against the spleen and the scurvy: Ale and beer brewed with these berries, being ripe, is an incomparable drink, familiar in Wales, where this tree is reputed so sacred that there is not a churchyard without one of them planted in it' (as among us the Yew).

SPARTIUM   There is only one species in this genus. It is *Spartium iunceum* or Spanish Broom. It flowers much later than our native

Broom, is taller, and the flowers individually are larger. It is a grand seaside plant and in a score of south coast resorts is seen and admired by thousands of holiday-makers. Probably many of them believe they are seeing only a well-grown specimen of our own Broom. I think that is what I thought when I first saw it at Torquay many years ago. Anyhow, they come, they see, they admire, but very rarely do they plant it in their gardens at home: it just is not seen in 'Codham, Cockridden and Childerditch' though it thrives anywhere and is good on chalk soils.

It is an ancient plant that has been known and respected for thousands of years. Dioscorides thought it had no leaves. Pliny described the ropes, mainly for marine cordage, that were made from the stems. It was in England before William Turner's day who found it 'in many gardines in Englande, in my Lordes gardine at Shene, and in my Lord Cobham's gardin a little from Graves End.' It was regarded with suspicion as a source of medicine but 'applied outwardly is found to helpe the *Sciatica* or pain of the hippes.'

SPIRAEA There is a lot of confusion over this genus because the flowers of some other families which are not related are very similar. Also the botanists have done a little rearranging, which makes for more uncertainty, especially in the herbaceous species. The tall plant with enormous pyramidal spires of summer flowers were *Spiraea aruncus*, but now the preferred name is *Aruncus sylvestris*. Some species have moved over to *Filipendula* and our Meadowsweet that was *Spiraea ulmaria* has become *Filipendula ulmaria*. All these are in the Rose family. The little pink or white Spiraea so much at home by the waterside is Astilbe and these are generally much smaller than Spiraeas. They are in the Saxifrage family. The ones we grow are garden hybrids from a mixed parentage of species such as *Astilbe japonica* and *A. sinensis*. To make things even more interesting there is a 6–8 foot tall plant related to Astilbe (or it was when I looked it up last!) and that is *Rodgersia aesculifolia*.

Now all this does not matter a fig to the gardener and I don't suggest anyone should remember it. But it raises an interesting point. Gardeners should beware of botany: it *could* drive them out of their gardens. Mind, a lot of botanists away from deciding about plant names are nice ordinary fellows like you and me.*

There are many species of shrub Spiraeas of which between, 30 and 40 are available and actually for sale.

For my taste two of these stand out. The first is *S. canescens* which sends up tall thin branches about 6 or 7 feet high. As these develop they arch outwards and in June and July are covered with flowers the whole length of the stems. The flowers are tiny but are carried in clusters, so many that the branches are solid with blossom. This is a most graceful and elegant shrub and it is very easy to grow anywhere. It deserves a place where it can be admired for the arching form. A young plant takes a few years to reach its best but it is completely reliable. New branches come up from the base every year and older ones should be cut out occasionally to make room for them.

My other favourite is *S. brumalda*. It does not grow very tall – about 3–4 feet – again in the form of a group of stems, each of which produces a flat head of deep pink flowers. *S. brumalda* is not always to be found in nurseries but a form called Anthony Waterer is, and this is even better than the species.† It is good anywhere but especially well suited to damp places and the waterside.

Of the others the following are the most commonly grown in gardens, *S. arguta* and *S. thunbergii* for spring flowering: for summer *S. nipponica*, *S. prunifolia* and *S. vanhoutii*.

SYMPHORICARPUS The common name is Snowberry and by this name it has been known since it was introduced from America nearly 200 years ago. It has the bad habit of sending up suckers far away and too freely. Apart from that it is a pretty little shrub with not very showy small flowers which bees love. It comes into leaf very early in the year, a fact noted by Cobbett who, it is said, was largely responsible for its becoming popular in English gardens. The flowers are followed by the white berries, small

---

* I'm not much better at pure grammar, apparently, than at pure botany!
† Always listed as a species but actually it is a hybrid.

marble size, that give it its common name. They are very ornamental but are often eaten by birds. Poultry will eat them. The shrub was widely grown once in cottage gardens and one of my childhood memories is of picking the berries from a thicket in our neighbours' farmyard and throwing them to the hens. They would come scuttling from all directions as soon as the distribution started, and I suppose I was amused to see the most dignified of them waddling along as fast as their legs could carry them. My kindness you will notice was not altogether disinterested! In country places the sites of long-vanished cottages can often be recognised by a group or old hedge of Snowberry.

I have made a little Symphoricarpus hedge in my garden and very neat and trim it is, for the slim branches are so easy to cut with shears or a sickle, while the electric trimmer goes over it in a matter of minutes. This generally means a poor show of berries. To get those, one shearing in early spring must be the full extent of pruning. But then it grows very tall – and it fans out. You can't have everything!

As for the suckers that come up some distance from the hedge I have not found them a great nuisance. They are easy to pull up or chop off, and it is possible to kill them with sodium chlorate without harming the parent plants. If they come up in grass the mower will keep them down.

There are a few species, some of which have coloured berries. The common Snowberry, probably the best, has a number of specific names. I believe the correct one is *S. albus*, but some lists may have *S. racemosus*. *S. orbiculatus* has pink berries, while there is a golden variegated form known as *S. orbiculatus variegatus*.

SYRINGA *Syringa vulgaris* is the Common Lilac. It has been grown in English gardens for hundreds of years. It is believed to be a native of eastern Europe but other species have come from India and northern India and some have wandered in from America. Although this easy fragrant shrub was the only variety grown for a long time, the introduction of new ones led to hybridising and, though many rarely set seed, enormous numbers of garden varieties have been raised and catalogued over the years. French gardeners have done most work on this genus and if you look up a list you have evidence of the fact in such titles as Ambassadeur, Capitaine Baltet, l'oncle Tom, Madame Lemoine and so on.

Madame Lemoine was the wife of Victor Lemoine, a famous nurseryman at Nancy, and he seems to have been the man who began the good work. Nancy was occupied during the Franco-Prussian War and he started his breeding experiments largely to occupy his time when so little else could be done.

Madame Lemoine – the Lilac not the lady – is still about the best of the double whites you can find. At least, it is my own favourite, though to me the scent is very weak.

Where so much is so good it is difficult to know what to praise as the best out of dozens or scores. This accumulation of kinds was no doubt very jolly when many gardens were vast and had much cheap labour to run them. Some catalogues still have a lot more choice than we need. I suppose that is better than having too little, but I think a number of nurseries are realising that too much is too much. I have a number of catalogues from first-class firms that have whittled down the choice (in other shrubs as well as Lilacs) to half a dozen or less.

The following can be recommended:

Etna. Single, deep purple.
Glory of Hortenstein. Single, purple red.
Souvenir de Louis Spath. Single, dark red. This has been a great
    favourite for the past 40 years.
Vestale. Single, white.
Here are some with double flowers:
Charles Joly. Dark red.
Katherine Havemeyer. Lavender.
Madame Lemoine. Pure white.
Michael Buchner. Lilac (in colour).
Mrs Edward Harding. Red.

Josiflexa Bellicent is a Canadian hybrid which bears large terminal Pannicles of pink flowers in June.

It used to be the practice to graft the hybrid Lilacs on stocks

Camellia Nagasaki growing in a border in a cool greenhouse

Variegated Dogwood, *Cornus variegata*, makes a good patch of colour in a far corner

of *S. vulgaris* or on Privet. Unfortunately these sucker badly and many gardeners know the curse of Lilac or Privet suckers coming up in thickets everywhere. Since they tend to shoot up on damaged places on the roots the more they are removed the faster they come. I find in my garden the best remedy is constant cutting with mower or a sickle. Many nurseries now send out Lilacs on their own roots and these are the ones to buy.

As a rule it is the named hybrids that are planted, but there are a lot of good species, or wild types, to choose from, though most small nurseries do not stock them. They are worth a place in any collection of shrubs. A full list is out of the question but here are a few that are suitable for most gardens.

S. chinensis. Sometimes called the Rowan Lilac. Deep lavender flowers. It is not a true species but generally listed as one.

S. josikaea. Hungarian Lilac. Violet in colour.

S. meyeri. Dwarf and purple.

S. pekinensis. White. Grows to tree size.

Gerard called the Lilac Pipe Privet: 'The later Physitians call the first Syringa, that is to say a Pipe because the stalkes and branches thereof when the pith is taken out are hollow like a Pipe: it is also many times syrnamed Candida or white, or Syringa Candida flore, or Pipe with a white floure, because it should differ from Lillach, which is sometimes named Syringa caerula or blew Pipe.'

He did not like the perfume. 'I once gathered the floures and layed them in my chamber window, which smelled more strongly after they had lien together a few houres, with such an un-acquainted savor that they awaked me out of sleepe, so that I could not rest till I had cast them out of my chamber.'

TAMARIX The Tamarisk was brought to this country from Germany, most likely by Bishop Grindal (later Archbishop of Canterbury) on his return at the end of Queen Mary's reign. There is another account that it was brought by 'the famous learned man William Turner Phisicion whiche doctor is a jewell among us English men . . . for his singular learning, knowledge and judgement.'

F

The Tamarisk is commonly thought of as a seaside shrub and indeed there it is invaluable for it cares not for the strongest gales, and salt in the wind has no effect on it. As single specimens or planted as windbreaks it is both ornamental and useful. But it is hardy and can be grown anywhere, and should be, again either for ornament or use. The branches are graceful and slender, the foliage much divided, something like that of Juniper; the 'plumose inflorescences' are pink or purple and cover the whole shrub like a cloud.

Any of the three species commonly offered is suitable for our gardens.

Tamarix gallica, sometimes called *T. anglica*, is the common European species. It has pink flowers. Isolated specimens will grow to tree size but can be kept shrubby by cutting back.

T. paviflora has pink flowers in May and decorative dark purple shoots.

T. pentandra is a late-flowering species. It bears a mass of feathery pink flowers.

T. pentandra rubra is the same but has red flowers.

Tamarisk has been a source of medicine for thousands of years. Pliny said an ointment made from the leaves was good for 'nightfoes or chilblanes' (I don't know whose translation that was). At one time it was thought to be the source of the Manna on which the Israelites fed in the wilderness. At certain seasons sap exudes from the plant; it crystallises into a sugary substance and falls. It must be collected before the sun melts it. The Arabs gather this as a sweetmeat. It corresponds reasonably well with the description of Manna given in *Exodus*.

In England in the Middle Ages it was used for 'treatment of the spleen'.

What jolly mistakes the herbalists of old must have had with their experiments. 'The Potecaries of Colon' said Turner, 'before I gave them warning used for thys, the Bowes of ughe.' (Yew)

And that would kill an elephant!

ULEX This is Gorse and I know not who, but I, would include it among popular shrubs. Yet a few seedlings arrived in my

garden and since they settled on a rough bit of ground, starved
by neighbouring trees, I let them stay and they have been worth
having. For small gardens I would say no, but for poor dry
corners in big ones or to cover a bit of the outskirts, or if you
should be near the sea or a cliff top then you could do worse than
plant a few *Ulex europaeus* or Common Gorse. There is a double
form *U. europaeus plenus* which has double flowers, also a dwarf
one *U. nanus*. As for its never being out of flowers – 'when the
Gorse is out of flower Kissing is out of fashion' – perhaps in a
mild district there may always be a flower or two on the bushes;
on my hillside, if the saying is true, then kissing is only fashionable
in high summer. The shrub is not very common on our hills, but
in the coastal areas I know best a hillside painted with the rich
yellow of *U. europaeus* is a sight to make your heart glad. They
say when Linnaeus had his first sight of an English hillside
covered with Gorse in full flower he fell on his knees and thanked
God for it. I have been told it was not Linnaeus but a German
botanist by the name of Dillenius. I don't see why they should
not both have thanked God.

A peculiarity of Gorse, or Furze or Whin, according to taste
or district, is the fierceness with which it burns. There must be a
very inflammable oil which remains in the dead wood, but I
cannot find that anyone has isolated it or said what it is. Really
dry Gorse will go up like a bomb at the first lick of a flame.
Centuries ago it was valued as fuel; according to Gerard: 'the
greatest and highest that I did ever see do grow about Excester in
the West parts of England, where the great stalkes are dearly
bought for the better sort of people, and the small thorny species
for the poorer sort.'

VERONICA These are sometimes listed as Hebe but in the Royal
Horticultural Society's Dictionary they are still under Veronica.
The shrub Speedwells are very good for seaside gardens, but a
bit tricky in cold climates. They will stand gales and salt winds
and not so much as drop a leaf and in inland gardens south of
the Thames are equally useful as at the seaside, even in exposed
places. They are beautiful as single specimens, good for hedges,

informal screens and ground cover; they prefer the open but are not bad in very light shade, say on the outskirts of woodland. There are all shapes, sizes and heights, but on the whole the best ones form rounded bushes in whose shade even Ground Elder (Goutweed) does not stand much chance. A number of the best are evergreen. The nurseries do not list all species as tender – there are about 30 or 40 garden varieties – and it may well be that we cold garden men are missing something good. Gardeners have always gone by what the older gardeners hand down as the voice of experience but which often is superstition and hearsay. Look at the exotics women are now managing as house plants, subjects which older gardeners said could only be managed in hothouses. More experimenting is needed. *Verbum sapientae*, which in case you have no more Latin than I (or Shakespeare: 'little Latin and less Greek') roughly means 'plant one and see.'

Veronica carnea definitely does seem to be tender. *V. bulkeana* which is claimed, with its long lavender-blue pannicles, to be the most beautiful of the genus, *V. veitchii* and *V. speciosa* are risky.

I feel like the waiter who ate up David Copperfield's pudding: 'oh-well-if-you-insist-on-planting-one' but if you *do* want to try the garden hybrids here is a selection that I think stands a good chance of success:

Alicia Amherst. A 4-foot shrub with deep purple flowers.
Autumn Glory. Violet flowers in autumn.
Eversley Seedling. Lilac flowers all summer.
Bowles hybrid. Lilac flowers, late flowering.
White Gem. Early flowering, white.

All those make bushes some 3 feet tall, perhaps the same through. A good tall variety is *V. paviflora* which can grow to as much as 6 feet.

V. armstrongii is a dwarf, suitable for the rock garden. The purple flower most commonly seen at the seaside is *V. elliptica latifolia*. It came to us from Chile but the others are natives of New Zealand. *V. elliptica* occasionally seeds itself, so watch for them. Who would miss a seedling or two? – so again to my scanty Latin: *verb. sap.*!

VIBURNUM This is a very large genus with two definite natives in it. The best known is *Viburnum opulus*, the Guelder Rose, though Gerard said it should be Elder Rose. Perhaps he was correct since before his time it was believed to be a kind of Elder. The Guelder may have come from the Dutch name of Gheldersche Roosen after the province of Gelderland. *V. opulus* is a good hedge plant having pretty flowers, first-rate leaf colour and attractive berries in autumn. But it is hardly a first-rate garden shrub, unless, as with many of what you could call border-line cases, there is a lot of space to be filled on the outskirts with poor soil in it. Then I can well imagine a group of Guelder Rose bushes giving a lot of pleasure. Seeing some marvellously rich coloured specimens in a Herefordshire hedge one sunny autumn morning I meant to go back later for some cuttings or a few rooted stems. I did not get round to doing it and just as well. My garden is full and I allow too many pensioners to stay because I do not like to turn them out. This personification of plants is a bit silly; if you are not careful it can get right out of hand. You know the sort of thing – 'seems a shame to throw away an old friend' – 'it enjoys a forkful of manure now and then' – and so on. Next thing is you are talking to them and passers-by are looking askance at you over the wall.

I have even known of a gardener who does talk to his plants. Incredible (or not?) but true.

'Look,' he says to the Apple, 'no fruit again this year. You'll have to do better than this or I'll get rid of you.'

It works. He said it did, anyhow. Do the plants really learn and inwardly digest, or is my friend even further into the lunatic fringe than the rest of us?

The Guelder Rose for the garden is the sterile form, *V. opulus sterile*. This is the Snowball Tree, a lovely little shrub, beloved of cottage gardens and worthy of a place anywhere. Those who do not know it can take the common name as its description. The heads of flowers are roughly tennis-ball size. The bush can grow rather lanky in time and stands pruning back after flowering as soon as it becomes awkwardly tall and bare at the base.

The other native is *V. lantana*, the Wayfaring Tree, which name may have been given to it by Gerard though Parkinson later said wayfarers got no pleasure from it. That was not quite fair since the autumn colour is brilliant. The blue-black berries also are attractive. But the Wayfaring Tree had better stay where the wayfarers can admire it, and that is in the hedgerows.

V. tinus, the Laurustinus, comes from the Mediterranean countries. It is in leaf a little like Bay and Portugal Laurel; was, in fact, once thought to be a sort of Laurel. It may be slightly tender. There is a difference of opinion on this point but on the whole it will stand most weathers. It will not, however, in my experience, flower as it should during the winter in the colder districts. But where the winters are warm, or in seaside gardens, the heads of blossom start to come out in autumn and go on appearing until spring. A lovely shrub. The berries of many of the Viburnums are edible. Those of *V. fragrans* are even a delicacy, so we are told, in China. But according to Parkinson those of the Laurustinus so burn and inflame the mouth and throat that it is insupportable. The cure was to hold milk in the mouth. W. E. Johns said of *V. opulus* that 'in Siberia the berries are made into paste with honey and flour and eaten as food but this is scarcely credible, so exceedingly offensive is the odour which they emit.'

V. tomentosum was the first of the oriental species to be grown here. It was introduced by Robet Fortune in the 1840s. This stands very high in the list of the most-desirable shrubs. It has striking form with a horizontal spread of branches. The flowers come in early summer and the autumn leaf colour is good. There are a few sub-species and garden forms, one, *plicatum* with snowball flowers. Otherwise the choice of variety is a matter of taste rather than virtue.

Later in the nineteenth century came *V. carlesii* and *V. fragrans*, the former from Korea, the latter from China. *V. carlesii* is a lovely spring-flowering shrub. I have had the late frosts nip the flowers on mine so in cold gardens a warm site would be a kindness. The flowers are pink in the buds, pure white when

fully open, and the fragrance is as pleasing as it is strong. Though
I cannot speak from experience I believe it is a good town plant,
doing well even in industrial districts. As ever the hybridists have
been at work and some very nice garden varieties have been
introduced. The poorest are no improvement on the type, and
the best are not so much better. The most outstanding is *V.
burkwoodii*, but I would choose *V. carlesii* in preference to *V.
carlcephalum* or *V. juddii* which are the best-known of its offspring.

The only thing to be wary of in *V. carlesii* is suckering.
Nurserymen graft it on a stronger-growing species, *V. lantana* by
the look of it. Almost always this produces a host of suckers and
if you do not cut them out promptly they will take over altogether.

V. fragrans is a gem. It starts to flower in autumn, giving its
best flush of bloom with me about mid-November. After that
there are occasional flower heads all through winter. Again we
have a shrub that is perfectly hardy but with flowers that do not
like severe frost. The first specimen I ever had was planted in the
open and I had few flowers or they were frost-browned. I moved
it to the shelter of an east wall (not exactly the warmest of places)
and after that it flowered profusely. Since then I have always
used it as a wall shrub. My present one also looks east and it is
embarrassingly vigorous. I am sorry I cannot quote experience
with a west or a south wall but my wall space is heavily booked.
The flower heads of *V. fragrans* come on the tips of shoots that
grow the previous summer so I encourage those and keep the
spread to reasonable proportions by cutting back fairly hard
when flowering is over.

Most of the other Viburnums are developments of, or closely
related to, those mentioned. *V davidii* is a 2-foot rounded evergreen bush; *V. hillieri* grows to 8 feet. But do not pay too much
attention to catalogue heights. I am sure my *V. fragrans* in its
sheltered corner is soaring far above the advertised stature. Some
of the species give a good show of berries, of which a few
apparently are edible. Farrar was promised seed of *V. fragrans* but
he said Yang Tusa, Prince of Jo-ni, and he quarrelled and the
Prince ate all the fruit and threw away the seeds. Parkinson's

warning has already been given: care is desirable if you are going to try any of the family.

One of the genus I have that is rather different from the others is *V. rhytidophyllum*. I am not sure whether it is beautiful or only strikingly different. It is a tall shrub, up to 10 feet and the leaves are large and long. They are very deeply veined, a rich deep green above, and very thickly furred with a sort of down underneath. They rather tend to catch the eye, are quite attractive, and of course very few people know the name. Who would, with a bundle of syllables like that? The flowers are a poorish white, the berries when they come – they don't always – are red turning black.

VINCA   This is the trailing blue Periwinkle. You would hardly think of this as a shrub, but it is. It has a very beautiful flower and since the best known are an excellent blue it is a wonder that it is not more widely grown. I suppose most gardeners think of it as a wild plant. So it is but it is none the worse for that and none the less worthy of a place in the garden. A bank of Periwinkle in full bloom is a fine sight indeed. To see it at its best it needs plenty of room to spread itself, but it is a most useful shrub in that it will grow and flower in shade. It makes good ground cover and being evergreen keeps most herbaceous weeds in order. The flowers start to come out in early summer and go on, to some extent, until September.

The best-known species is *Vinca major*, and a few cuttings of that or even a rooted piece or two can be gathered from banks and hedges. *V. minor* is smaller, lies down flat on the job, though so does *V. major*. I have no plants of *V. minor* for comparison. According to Mr Keble Martin *V. major* is a sub-species of *V. minor*. The latter might make an attractive pocket at the back of a rock garden.

There are variegated-leaf forms of both, and another, much less desirable to my taste, with pale lavender flowers, also a rather pretty one with white flowers.

But to quote Southey in a different sense from what he intended, 'Blue, darkly, deeply beautifully blue.' The blue

Periwinkle is always the best. And – this has nothing to do with shrubs – Southey wasn't *always* as bad a poet as he is made out to be.

Culpeper said 'the Leavs eaten by Man and Wife together, causeth Love between them.'

That's useful to know!

VITIS* The Vine deserves a book all to itself. After all, for good or evil it has for thousands of years been grown and cultivated, revered and hated, loved and abused. It has been a comfort and a curse, a solace and a destroyer. You can belong to the school who quote 'Use a little wine for thy stomach's sake and thine often infirmities' or hold that 'Wine is a mocker, strong drink is raging.'

We can be drinkers or teetotal: the Bible backs up both of us.

There is an old legend that the Devil buried a lion, a lamb and a hog under the first Vine planted by Noah. As a result men, after drinking wine, are as brave as a lion, as mild as a lamb, or wallow in the mud.

When you come to think of it that sums up the truth out of the contradictory feelings men have had about this useful and pleasant, but dangerous plant. As usual you find the truth in the fairy-tale!

Of the fruiting Vine, *Vitis vinifera*, as an English shrub, the facts are in rather a muddle. Tacitus said that the Vine and the Olive would not grow in England. Yet the colonising Romans, perhaps missing their easy wine, made an attempt to cultivate grapes. Undoubtedly the Vine was grown in many places. Centuries after the Romans, monasteries had their vineyards. If the sites are examined you can see the terraced layout where they were, as you can at Hereford. And Hereford is well to the north for Vine growing. Vine Street is named after the vineyards of Ely. And so on. The evidence for English vineyards is everywhere if we look for it.

Grapes will *grow* in this country. I have seen a Thames-side house at Oakley Green near Windsor where hot-house grapes

* The ornamental vines have been dealt with under Ampelopsis.

outlived the hot-houses and flourished mightily in the open. But there is a difference between growing them and ripening them. Grapes do not ripen well or consistently in this country. So what might well have happened in those forgotten vineyards was that the wine makers used the fruit unripe, which you *can* do.

When foreign (or better) wine was available cheaply, then the native grapes would be neglected.

In a warm and sheltered garden a crop of grapes can be ripened when September and October are warm and not too damp. I would not like to depend on them for my living, though. I remember, when I was a boy, being given a large bunch from a very sheltered walled garden in Pembrokeshire. They were as sweet as sugar. How well I remember! Such delicacies did not come to small boys too frequently in those days.

Gardeners in warm places or owning a cold greenhouse might like to try a Vine. There are four good varieties that could yield good fruit *and* the satisfaction of growing something their neighbours would not have.

Brandt has reddish-black grapes. There is a bonus of brilliant leaf colour in autumn. Dutch Sweetwater is I believe the easiest. The fruit is greenish-white and sweet. I have an idea that this may be the one the gardener at Colby Lodge gave me in one of his generous moods. *Vitis vinifera incana* is the Dusty Miller grape. The leaves are covered with a white cobweb down and the grapes are black. *V. vinifera purpurea* is sometimes called the Teinturier grape. It is noted for its richly-coloured leaves.

WEIGELA   This is often found in lists as Diervilla, but there is little consistency in the catalogues. I think, at the moment, the botanists have put the two together. Dierville came first; he sent an American species home from Canada about 1700. von Weigel (1748–1831) was honoured by having the Asiatic species named after him. By the rule that says the earliest name shall be used it seems as though Diervilla should be used. So gardeners, always as contrary as Mary in *her* garden, use Weigela.

The shrub is related to the Honeysuckles and the flowers have a Honeysuckle scent. The flowers could be likened to large

Honeysuckle trumpets or as one grower suggests, to Foxgloves. Most kinds are about 3 feet to 4 feet tall. They spread into bushes which in early summer are covered with red or reddish trumpets. The American species are not grown much, if at all, nowadays. There are some half-dozen Asiatic species, mostly from China or Korea, but on the whole it is best to choose from the garden varieties on sale. These are easy and reliable and very showy when in bloom. The following are among the best:

Abel Carrière, rose-coloured with large flowers; Bristol Ruby, red; Conquête, large pink flowers; Eva Rathke, crimson, late flowering; Gustave Mallet, rose colour; La Perle, white flowers flushed with pink.

WISTERIA What you like best is a matter of taste. One man's mother-in-law is another man's poison, as our roadman says. But there is no doubt that to the majority of us the Wisteria is way out ahead of all the other flowering shrubs. Yet the strange thing is that in the majority of gardens it is never planted. There seems to be a superstition that it is difficult. It certainly is not. It is one of the easiest of shrubs. It likes sunshine and it likes plenty of room. It grows very vigorously so does well in a good soil, though it will do well in any so long as it gets nourishment in the form of mulches of manure and compost, supplemented occasionally in early spring with a handful or two of general fertiliser.

It *is* slow sometimes to get started. I had that trouble myself. The reason is that, as many wall shrubs do, it gets planted close to the wall and such places are often bone-dry half the time. Any wall shrub should be watered in its early days. The Wisteria, though, makes a vigorous root system and once the roots make their way to the open garden they find also their share of moisture. In its early days once I had guessed why it was slow I often watered mine. Now it is growing heartily I do not bother.

Training is simple. If you plant it as a wall climber it will make its own way very nicely, thank you, if it has anything to twine around. If there is no means of support then something must be supplied in the form of a few wires or a length of narrow netting. The green plastic-covered netlon is excellent, or anything else you fancy. Train somewhat after the Vine fashion. That is, select a few rods as the main framework and arrange them in the direction and position you want. These can go as far as you like – often they will go further! – then you nip the side shoots to a few buds. The short side stems will produce flowering spurs.

One warning: if you have a nice crop of buds which begin to fall when they should be forming the racaemes (chains) of flowers, the plant almost certainly lacks water. Do not over-water immediately but give one fair soaking and then a little at a time. Too much drink is as bad as too little – same as with humans!

If there is no wall available very lovely bushes can be grown by training over old, unwanted, or even dead trees. The same principles apply as for wall specimens: sunshine, plenty of good soil, adequate moisture.

In some gardens a Wisteria is grown as a standard shrub. To do this it must be kept to a single stem, tied in to a strong stake. It is stopped (cut off) at the required height and the shoots that follow have to be trained, often over some sort of iron framework. Personally, I do not care for these as much as for one that has been allowed to wander at its own sweet will over an old tree, though when standards are exhibited at one of the big shows they are always greatly admired.

The first Wisteria to be grown in England was brought from America about 1725 and was called the Carolina Kidney Bean. This never became very popular, but the Chinese species we grow now, *Wisteria sinensis*, was described at about the same time by a French missionary. It was known here by repute for a long time but it was 1816 before plants reached us. They were grown in various botanical gardens with success, but do not seem to have got into the gardens of the general public. Perhaps that is how the shrub got its reputation for being difficult. It was seen and admired but it was not available. The R.H.S. had one about 160 feet from end to end, and I believe Kew's specimen, planted some time in the mid-nineteenth century, is still flourishing. The largest I ever saw was on an inn wall at Chateaubriand, a little town in Normandy, or it might be Brittany. It had a trunk the size of a small tree. The inn did not so much support the shrub as the shrub supported the inn. The place could not have fallen down if it had wanted to.

Wisterias are easy to propagate from layers. Mostly the branches are too high to be pegged to the ground or into a flower-pot but it is easy to untie a shoot or two and let them grow earthwise. With Wisteria plants fetching some thirty or more shillings each at the present time, a few spares, for free, is quite an idea. A healthy little Wisteria would be a welcome birthday or Christmas present for any gardener.

Or they could be distributed regardless of season to Wisteria-less gardens. Then we should see more of them.

There are some half-dozen species and sub-species. The most popular is *W. sinensis* (or *chinensis*). The flowers are lavender in colour, fragrant (though grown out of reach of most noses) borne on racaemes (Laburnum fashion) some 8 to 12 inches long. I have found the shade to be slightly variable, so if you have any preference for a light or a dark colour it is advisable to visit the nursery when the flowers are out.

W. alba is a white form, while there are double flowers on *W. sinensis flore-pleno*. *W. floribunda* (or *multijuga*) has very long racaemes, over 2 feet long in some cases, and this also has a white form. *W. floribunda rosea* is pink. *W. venusta* is white, very similar to the white form of *W. sinensis*.

Chapter 8: SHRUBS THAT ARE NOT WELL KNOWN

Every one knows the shrubs that are commonly grown and which may be found in any garden. They are recognised by sight if not by name. Outside what might be called the familiar inhabitants of the shrub garden there is a small multitude (if that is not too contradictory) that is less familiar and a few that could be called entirely unknown. Some of these are hardly worth growing except perhaps by dedicated collectors; there are others which are beautiful and desirable, but are, on the whole, over-looked or neglected.

There are reasons for this. A few of them are difficult to grow anywhere, but the most usual reason for omitting them is that they are very often not hardy. In the extreme south, to some extent south of the Thames, winters are relatively short if not sweet. On the south coast, in spite of freak weather from time to time, frost is not a menace, though we can none of us anywhere rely on complete safety and even in favoured Cornish valleys and sheltered Devon coombes calamities have overtaken cherished treasures from time to time. But growing something tender down there is worth a risk, and sometimes is no risk at all.

To those of us who garden where a mild winter is a mercy and a memory to be cherished, a lot of lovely shrubs are just not possible. The realist recognises the fact and does not attempt the impossible. Some failures in any garden are inevitable; no point then in courting them. The decision must be made when to be cautious and when it is worth being bold and trying an experiment.

Here is offered a list of shrubs that are not very well known. If you are in the warm south there may be a few you would like to grow. Elsewhere if you have a warm garden, a walled garden, a sheltered garden not troubled by cold drying winds or severe recurring frosts you may care to chance your luck. Most of these are worth having, but only if you can have them at their best.

ABELIA A member of the Honeysuckle family bearing flowers mainly white or in pink shades. *Abelia triflora* with scented flowers is a good wall shrub for mild districts.

ABUTILON This is often grown in greenhouses but sometimes seen on a south wall. The flowers are trumpet or bell shaped, red or orange. You often see some good specimens on walls or by porches in places like Normandy and Brittany.

ARUNDINARIA Not really a shrub at all but a grass. It is one of the Bamboos. It is often used as a shrub and *Arundinaria vagans*, the smallest species, makes good ground cover. All the Bamboos are of doubtful hardiness, but this genus succeeds in most gardens and is excellent at or near sea level.

AUCUBA The Aucuba is perfectly hardy. It is an evergreen shrub something like a Laurel; the flowers are poor but in some species the berries make a good show. It is an excellent shrub for poor soils and for shade but can hardly be classed as a choice plant. Some species have variegated leaves.

CAMPSIS Also known as Bignonia or the Trumpet Climber this is very good for a warm wall. The flowers, trumpet shaped, grow in clusters and come out in late summer in orange or red shades. *Campsis grandiflora* (*chinensis*) needs some support; *C. radicans* has aerial roots.

CARYOPTERIS These are small shrubs something like Verbena. They do best in full sun in a warm corner, and in such a spot I have grown one for years in my own garden. The flowers are blue.

CERCIS This is the Judas Tree, so called because it is the tree (or one of them!)* on which Judas hanged himself. It is quite hardy but must come in this section because it grows to tree size. The flowers are purple, pea-type and most attractive and the leaves are pretty. The two species, *Cercis racemosa* and *C. siliquastrum*, are

* See Elder.

worth growing as specimens or as hedge trees. *C. siliquastrum* is the better because it flowers quite freely while young.

CHIMONANTHUS Sometimes called Wintersweet it seems to be hardy but is best grown as a wall plant. It has flowers of a shape almost impossible to describe – like bits of rag or shreds of coloured paper. They come out in mid-winter and are among the most fragrant shrubs we have. *Chimonanthus fragrans* is the best species. Young plants do not always flower freely.

CHOISYA *Choisya ternata*, an evergreen, is called the Mexican Orange Blossom. It has white scented flowers all spring and summer. It is easy in some gardens but of doubtful hardiness.

CLERODENDRON This bears white scented flowers in late summer and early autumn, then blue berries. Easy, but grows to tree size.

CLETHRA *Clethra arborea* has flowers like Lily-of-the-Valley and they are scented. It is a tender shrub and the Clethras are all for lime-free soils. *C. alnifolia* and *C. barbinervis* are sometimes included with hardy shrubs, a listing that is more hopeful than certain, but if the nurseries can manage them so can we.

COLUTEA This is the Bladder Senna with yellow pea-style flowers followed by big inflated pods. It is an easy shrub, good for an odd corner, but it is not exactly an aristocrat.

COROKIA A small evergreen shrub with a mass of crooked stems. It is curious rather than a rare beauty. It bears yellow starry flowers in May with perhaps some red berries to follow.

CORYLOPSIS This is related to Hamamelis, or Witch Hazel, but the flowers are bell-shaped. They are yellow and scented. The shrub seems to be hardy; sad to say the flowers which come out in early spring, are not.

DESFONTAINEA This is an evergreen, holly-leaf shrub that has tubular scarlet yellow flowers in late summer. It is a native of Chile and Peru and is not hardy.

EMBOTHRIUM A lovely shrub with brilliant honeysuckle flowers of an orange-scarlet shade. It needs lime-free soil and is far from hardy.

ENKIANTHUS Hardy, but requires a lime-free soil. It has pretty cup-shaped, drooping flowers in summer, but its greatest attraction is the rich autumn leaf colour.

EXOCHORDA I have not grown this but one catalogue I have says it is not suitable for chalky soil; another says it does well on chalk. So whichever type of soil you have it seems worth a try. Only half of us can lose our money. Long arching branches bear large white flowers in early summer.

GAULTHERIA It is related to the Heathers, hates lime, needs woodland conditions and a cool rootrun. Very nice but rather temperamental. Gardeners who have the right conditions should try it. The flowers are followed by berries which are supposed to be edible. *Gaultheria procumbens* is the Partridge Berry.

GREVILLEA This is not very hardy and does not like lime or shallow soils. The flowers, either red or yellow, are more curious than beautiful.

KOLKWITZIA *Kolkwitzia amabilis* is very closely related to Weigela but has rather smaller flowers. It deserves a place in any garden, though it is doubtful if it is worth growing as well as Weigela.

LAVATERA Another Tree Mallow. This is a native and can be found growing wild at the seaside. The Hollyhock flowers are pink. This is hardly a shrub for the best positions but would be a useful stalwart for an odd corner. It grows best in sunshine, but as far as I know is hardy.

LEYCESTERIA Not particularly popular; not particularly beautiful either. A useful shrub for the edge of woodland. It has 6-foot, dark green stems and claret-coloured bracts round the white flowers in late summer.

MUTISIA This is hardly ever seen in gardens. An evergreen, it is a true climber, with tendrils, so may deserve more notice as evergreen climbers are not common. The flowers are Daisy-like in pinkish shades. Two species are available, *Mutisia ilicifolia* and *M. oligodon*, both from South America.

PASSIFLORA The Passion Flower caused a sensation when it was introduced to Europe from Brazil about 1610 by Jacomo Bosio who was writing a book of the Cross of Calvary. Every part of the flower seemed so much a symbol of some part of the Passion of our Lord that it appeared miraculous. In a way it was.

Here is Bosio's description:

'The filaments resemble a blood-coloured fringe, as though suggesting the scourge with which our blessed Lord was tormented. The column rises in the middle. The nails are above it; the crown of thorns encircles the column; and close in the centre of the flower from which the column rises is a portion of a yellow colour, about the size of a *reale*, in which are five spots or stains of the hue of blood, evidently setting forth the five wounds received by our Lord on the Cross.

'The crown itself is surrounded by a kind of veil, or very fine hair, of a violet colour, the filaments of which number seventy-two, answering to the number of thorns with which, according to tradition, our Lord's crown was set.'

He goes on to compare the leaves with the head of a spear, the spots on the underside of them with the thirty pieces of silver.

Silly, I suppose. Yet rather odd, to say the least. The plant was flowering long before the Crucifixion. Was Bosio childish – or childlike? Ah well . . . *Except ye become as little children* . . .

Passiflora caerulea is the species grown for its flowers; if you want fruit you must grow *P. edulis*. I have planted both in a cold greenhouse, without any great success, but I admit I was not trying. The house was over-full and new plants to try were at that time not being welcomed with enthusiasm. I have seen good specimens in the south and there was one growing over a cottage in South Morton in Berkshire which sprawled over the thatched roof and you could hardly open a window without a Passion Flower staring you in the face. Very nice too!

The fruits of two other species are the Granadillas but you won't find those in many, if any, English gardens.

PERNETTYA This is a showy dwarf evergreen, grown for its lovely berries of many shades from white to dark purple. It is a delightful little shrub for completely lime-free soil. It likes a cool root-run.

PHLOMIS Jerusalem Sage is *Phlomis fruticosa*, an evergreen with woolly leaves and yellow sage-like flowers arranged in whorls through summer. Easy in poor soil, it is not much seen, which is a pity as it is a good stand-by for some of the more difficult sites. It is slightly tender but in all except the very coldest gardens will grow up again after being cut back by frost. It is good by the sea and salt winds have little effect on it.

PHYGELIUS Phygelius is a small shrub with flowers something like Pentstemon. An easy plant in mild gardens though even in them a sheltered wall is considered the best position. My own experience of it is that it lives through the worst of our Welsh winters, but apparently it does not like them because it flowers only rarely.

PIERIS This is a beautiful and choice shrub once called Andromeda and under that name it may still be found in some lists. The white flowers, bell-like, hang in clusters, almost grape-like in their profusion.

It is not easy. The soil must be free of lime, peaty and moist and the position lightly shaded. In addition, if there are spring frosts the flowers will be damaged. It is a very worth-while shrub if it can enjoy the right conditions. There are half a dozen species, all good. *Pieris forrestii* is about the best with which to start.

PITTOSPORUM Another good shrub but really not hardy enough even for a wall except in the warmest places. *Pittosporum tenuifolium* is grown in a few places in Cornwall for its foliage. The flowers are not showy but are scented.

RUSCUS Butcher's Broom, a berrying shrub, curious more than beautiful. The apparently pointed leaves are flattened stems which carry insignificant flowers. There are male and female plants and both are needed before the bushes will set a crop of berries. Mr Keble Martin lists it as a native, mainly of southern England. I have been told it got its name because butchers used the wood for their skewers.

SARCOCCA *Sarcocca humilis* is an attractive small shrub with insignificant flowers but pretty berries. It is easy and worth growing more widely. Height ranges from 1 to 2 feet. *S. hookeriana* and *S. ruscifolia* are taller, up to 4 feet.

SOBARIA This genus is in appearance very like Spiraea, in fact where it is grown it is generally called Spiraea. It can be distinguished by the pinnate leaves. *Sobaria aitchisoni* and *S. arborea* are both handsome. They need a rich soil.

TRICUSPIDARIA It is often listed as Crinodendron. It comes from Chile and is a beauty. The flowers have been compared to crimson lanterns hanging along the branches. Alas, they will not hang there for most of us because the whole shrub is notoriously tender.

VACCINUM Our native Bilberry is a Vaccinum. So far as I can make out this is synonymous with Winberry and Whortleberry. *Vaccinum oxycoccus* is the Cranberry. These are hardly garden shrubs but if you do happen to have a bit of peaty ground where little else grows they would make good ground cover, and I feel they might make good undercover for bog gardens, in which some of the coarser grasses have a nasty habit of taking over.

In Radnor and Brecon, perhaps in other Welsh counties, the Winberry harvest, even up to the last war, was quite an important event. Whole families went out to the Winberry hills and the berries when sold added quite a lot to many a modest income. In those days the Welsh spas were crowded and there was a great demand for this unusual fruit. Many children made enough money every year to buy a complete outfit of clothes. I don't *think* modern children are usually as ambitious or as determined, but a day on the Winberry hills can still be a profitable sort of picnic.

YUCCA You either like the Yucca very much or despise it very much. It can hardly be overlooked. At my seaside home there were a lot of them in the churchyard. Now what happened is curious because there was a much-respected superstition in Pembrokeshire that if you took anything, plants or flowers, out of the churchyard, disaster, usually a death in the family, followed. But we boys used to cut the pointed leaves and use them as swords. I am sure we took them without the slightest dread of the doom to come. And it is a wonder doom did not come for those leaves were sharper than Goliath's spear, and board hard. No doubt a battle was followed by a few sore behinds, but I remember nothing worse!

The great spires of creamy flowers of Adam's Needle, *Yucca gloriosa*, is an imposing sight. Very lovely and yet . . . so much flower! If you can't have too much of a good thing you can certainly have rather a lot of it.

ZENOBIA This also could have been entered as Andromeda, but who could resist being able to make an entry under Z! *Zenobia pulverulenta* is a beautiful 6-foot shrub bearing, in summer, flowers similar to Lily-of-the-Valley. It is hardy but must have a cool moist root-run and the soil should not contain even a trace of lime.

The shrub is named in honour of Zenobia, Queen of a short-lived kingdom, Palmyra, situated in the Syrian Desert. She succeeded her husband on the throne, defied Rome and was defeated by Aurelian (AD 273) and taken back to Italy where she was led in a triumphal procession. But her chains were of gold for she was a descendant of Cleopatra and, they say, even more beautiful. She lived the rest of her life with her children in a beautiful villa by the Tiber.

Who remembers her romantic story now? Well, if we plant *Z. pulverulenta* it might remind us what happened to a beautiful woman who let ambition outrun discretion. There is a moral in that and having been brought up on Aesop I like to finish with a moral!

INDEX